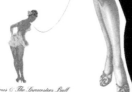

I Don't Take Requests

DJ Fat Tony
with Michael Hennegan

CORONET

First published in Great Britain in 2022 by Coronet
An Imprint of Hodder & Stoughton
An Hachette UK company

3

A CIP catalogue record for this title is available from the British Library

Hardback ISBN 9781529389449
eBook ISBN 9781529389456

Typeset in Meridien by Palimpsest Book Production Ltd, Falkirk, Stirlingshire

Printed and bound in Great Britain by Clays Ltd, Elcograf S.p.A.

Hodder & Stoughton policy is to use papers that are natural, renewable
and recyclable products and made from wood grown in sustainable forests.
The logging and manufacturing processes are expected to conform to
the environmental regulations of the country of origin.

Hodder & Stoughton Ltd
Carmelite House
50 Victoria Embankment
London EC4Y 0DZ

www.hodder.co.uk

This book is dedicated to unconditional love,
to my dog Tailor who never judged. To my mum
and all the mothers of the world. To anyone who
has struggled with addiction and for anyone who has
found recovery in any way, shape or form.

IF THERE WAS A LINE BETWEEN RIGHT AND WRONG,
I SNORTED IT YEARS AGO

Prelude

I'm pretty sure I'd already shat myself that night. I say shat myself, but by that stage of a bender it would just be something like water. And I say night, but by day five of rollercoasting – freebasing eight-balls of coke and then taking three or four Rohypnol or diazepam at a time to take the edge off the paranoia and psychosis – day and night had lost all context. A day could be seventy-two hours and the only way I vaguely kept track was by which club night we were at.

Everything had got out of control – the drugs, the sex, the money – everything. When I was high I would just have guys over all day long, one after the other after the other. It was never messy on the first night, or too bad on the second, to be honest, but by the third or the fourth, things would really have started to fall apart. All my limbs were aching from dehydration and I literally couldn't move my fingers. I was so emaciated that you could close your hands around my entire waist. I had one tooth left and was in constant pain with my jawbone, which was crumbling away. I'd run out of crystal meth two weeks earlier – the guy that brought it over for me from New York hadn't managed to bring me more, but by God, I'd done every other drug I could get my hands on.

It was the week after my thirty-ninth birthday, I'd had a party at the Egg Club on the Friday and we'd been on a roll from there. I didn't need a constant crew – I could find one, put them down and pick another up. I also had no problem bowling up to a club on my own. I'd been at Fabric on the Sunday night and was so dehydrated that I'd been putting petroleum jelly all over my face – round my lips, on my eyelids. I'd rub it all over because everything was just so dry – I was like an Egyptian mummy. I swear I don't think I drank a glass of water for about eight years. I thought that because I drank Jack Daniels with ice that would do the job. You could pull at my skin and it would stay upright like cardboard. There was a group of people at the bar in Fabric doing sambuca shots. 'Oi! Give me one of those!' But the barman wouldn't give me one, so I reached over and snatched a glass as he lit them, necked it and my whole face caught alight because of the paraffin in the jelly. I ran through the club with my whole fucking face on fire – I burnt my hair and my eyebrows off, and I still didn't give a fuck. From there, I went on to a pub across the road in Smithfield Market and then to my dealer's warehouse, did more of everything and rolled around on his floor wrapped in a rug for three days. Pretty standard.

There were still a few people booking the Tony show, some out of loyalty in the hope that I might manage to keep it together if I knew I had to turn up to a gig, some because they knew that people would turn up to watch the car crash. And so I was sitting in the back room of The Cross club waiting to DJ after nearly a week-long bender. I was a zombie, the lights were out and I was rocking back and forth, wringing my hands and chewing my gums. My friend Edna ran in to tell me that my boyfriend Johnny was there. Our relationship by that point was as turbulent and toxic as they come. I'd cheated on him with pretty much every guy in London and as a result most of our interactions now were physical; there wouldn't be black eyes but there was so much anger there that I just remember thinking, *Christ, I can't fucking deal with this right now.* I was just about holding it together. I'd gone back to the flat earlier in the day and taken his Fake London jeans without asking and thought he was coming to drag them off my legs. I just couldn't deal with it.

My body froze as he came in, every muscle tensed; the very last reserves of any senses I had were saying I was in for a fight. Johnny stopped and looked me up and down, his eyes full of sadness and a softness I hadn't seen for a long time. 'Tony, are you all right?' he said, and the kindness threw me. Then he said it again: 'Are you all right?'

'What?' I mumbled. I felt like the walls were closing in around me, rushing towards me and down on me in waves.

'What happened to you, Tony? Where did you go?' And something broke, deep inside. I started crying, huge, overpowering, chest-heaving, body-shaking sobs, and they wouldn't stop.

Please, get me out of here.

1.

The Quiet Life

My poor fucking mother. Seriously. I came out of the womb causing drama. She fell down the stairs a month before I was due, was rushed to hospital and I made my entrance into the world feet first, after a respectable twelve-hour labour, at 11am on 25 November 1965.

From there we went home to 78 Denbigh Street in Pimlico, South London, just a few streets from where I live now, fifty-seven years later. By all accounts the first two years of my life were pretty plain sailing. 'You were such a good baby,' my mum likes to say, 'I even had to wake you up for feeds.' My mum Dawn was the most glamorous person I knew growing up. When I was born my mum had this huge beehive hair; by the 70s she had a mass of permed curls. She would always dress up, she did her hair every day, she always had her make-up just right and would always wear chic clothes and would always be in fashion. She loved all of that stuff.

When I was two I went into hospital with a collapsed lung and stayed there for two weeks. 'Oh, you loved the attention you got on that ward,' my mum says, 'you had them wrapped around your little finger.' After that, the London air was deemed too dirty for me so I was sent to stay with my Nanny Surman – my mum's mum – in Kent for six months. She was a headmistress and was absolutely fucking terrifying, but I remember loving having her all to myself. 'I think that's when your personality really started to develop,' my mum says now. 'You were like a different child when you came back.' Now, looking back, I kind of think that's where the monster was born.

'Take. Him. Back.' These were my first words when I met my little brother Dean, who arrived next. Talk about a fucking welcome. Because my mum didn't have just me to deal with, there were three of us, with exactly four years between each one. Me, Dean and my older brother Kevin, and we were a lot for anyone to deal with. Dean had a strangulated hernia of the testicles when he was born and was taken back into hospital a few days later. I thought they'd actually done what I'd asked and taken him back. I was thrilled. Sadly, he was back within a week. Little fucker. I was terrible, though, I used to move the pram when he was sleeping and put it under the phone that was plugged into the wall and wait for it to ring and wake him up. He would start screaming and then my mum would shout: 'What the hell are you doing putting him there?' 'He likes it,' I'd say, looking as angelic as possible.

It was a pretty normal childhood. We lived on an estate in Battersea, but it was a nice, new estate, I can't ever remember having to go without. My mum worked on the Buckingham Palace estate as a cleaner and then went on to become a supervisor at the palace itself. I remember thinking what she did was quite cool – she definitely thought it was glamorous. My dad Michael was a plumber and had his own business. He was a huge, terrifying man. Six foot one, and built like a brick shit house, he had hands like spades and fingers like bananas, and he wasn't afraid to use force when it came to us boys. He was so strict. Now I realise he just came from a different time – his dad was a sergeant major with the Scots Guards and that's just how he'd been brought up. My dad was the first person to have a satellite dish on our estate. He was 'Top-of-the-range Mike'. Everything would have to be the best, but he worked hard and he wanted nice things. That's just how he was. We always had a good stereo in the house and I remember we'd wake up on a Sunday morning to him playing Roy Orbison, Elvis, the Royal Teens, Jim Reeves. One of the first things I can remember is music being on in the house, and my mum dancing around making the lunch.

I was a total mummy's boy, right from the start. If I could be by her side then I would be. I was a very snuggly child. She would always wear perfume; I don't know which one, but she always had an underlying smell of Oil of Ulay, and I remember the jar of it being in the bathroom. We always had pets – we had this big Old English Sheepdog called Worthington who we all loved. There was a lot of love in our house growing up. But even back then, I remember not being able to accept it. Birthdays, for instance, were amazing. Every kid from the estate would be around and my aunts and cousins and all my mum's friends and their kids – you were the total star of the show for the day. You would have thought I'd have loved that, right? But I couldn't accept that love. Even then I'd try my best to throw a spanner in the works. It's a hard thing to explain. My dad had very rigid boundaries, and was really tough with us after my little brother came along, for some reason I felt abandoned and unloved.

I'd always act up around my birthday. One of my birthday tricks was to start dropping hints of what I wanted six months before the day because I knew my mum would order it from the catalogue and pay for it weekly. Then a few days before my birthday I'd put a notice on my bedroom door saying that I didn't want that gift anymore – let's say it was roller skates – and I wanted a new bicycle instead. The notice went something like this: 'Dear Mum, Dad, Kevin and Dean, just so you know I've changed my mind. I no longer want X and now want Y. If you haven't managed to get it for me by my birthday then you can take it to the poor kids down the street and cancel celebrating at all. I won't be coming out of my room all day.' It meant I always got the present I'd asked for originally and the new one too. All children are manipulative but some are better than others. I remember thinking I was fucking A-star. Not a lot has changed on that front, if I'm honest.

Sundays were special. My nan would come round for a Sunday lunch, my dad would go and collect her and we'd all sit around the table and eat a Sunday roast together. Teatime would be tinned salmon and tomato sandwiches with loads of vinegar on, followed by fruit cake. It was family bliss, you couldn't ask for more. I miss those days and the simplicity of it.

Weekday dinner times at home were hectic – with three boys we would bicker and fight non-stop. Oh my God, would we. My mum would always cook and we were made to sit at the table and wait while my dad had his served to him in front of the telly – Sunday was the only day he sat with us as a family. My mum made a great toad-in-the-hole and rice pudding. She loved a Vesta curry out of a box on a Saturday night. It was a sort of dried curry with dried rice and you'd add water to it all and cook it. Sounds grim but this was the 70s. I loved them.

My dad was a man of two sides. He was a good-looking man; he was a rocker and had this jet-black quiff all of his life. Like I said, he was six foot one, so with the quiff he was huge, and he was forceful; you didn't mess with him. If someone started a fight with my dad he'd batter everyone, he wouldn't stop until he'd won. My little brother is the same; recently some kid sent his daughter a nasty text, so my brother went round, had it out with the dad and then said, 'Sort your fucking son out.' That was my dad. On the estate growing up you just did not fuck with Mick Marnoch.

We were all terrified of him – especially on a Saturday night after he'd been in the pub all day. We would have had the day to entertain ourselves and so would be on fine waggish form by the time he got back and would often overstep the mark. We would lock ourselves in the bedroom and hide when we knew we were in trouble but he would punch holes through the door and get the belt out on us. That wasn't the worst of it, though; it was really bad when my mum got involved.

They would have gone down to the pub, my dad would have one too many Scotches and they would invite people back to the house. There would be an argument and my dad would carry on drinking, and then my mum would get involved and start nagging him, end up throwing something at him and then my dad would lose his rag. Scotch did not agree with my father, it was the chemical that gave him that mental imbalance. Some people get it with white wine or vodka, my dad got it with Scotch.

There were never any arguments or any nastiness without Scotch whisky. My dad could drink beer until the cows came home and be fine but add whisky to the mix and it ended badly; a row would escalate to boiling point and then he would lash out. More than once I had to take my mum to the hospital to have her stomach pumped after she'd taken an overdose when they'd had a fight. I remember another time her saying she was going to do it and giving me all her jewellery. I would have been about nine or ten. It's a really traumatic thing for a kid to witness. I'd have to call my dad and tell him that my mum was in hospital and he'd rush over and they'd make up. But for all their faults, they loved each other. No one stays together for forty years without really loving each other. My dad looked after my mum, there was a respect there, and in return my mum looked after my dad. She loved to cook and keep the house together for him, and he loved to buy gifts in return; she always wanted shoes and bags and she had no problem with him buying her a bit of jewellery.

My brothers and I were terrors growing up and to keep the three of us in check took a lot of force. All of us were off-the-scale ADHD. I've never been tested but I'm sure I've got it, and the same with dyslexia. My attention span is terrible – one minute I'll be able to focus and the next minute I'm onto something else.

My older brother Kevin was in trouble from as young as I can remember – first it was nicking from the local shop, then it moved on to stealing from the toy shop. I remember my granddad piling everything Kevin had stolen up in the garden and setting fire to it while we watched – I'm not really sure what that was meant to teach us. And that was just the start of the problems with Kevin.

Even as a young child, I was always in trouble, too. We'd have to take it in turns to have new school shoes, but I'd go out and wreck mine on purpose so that I could get a new pair again. But it was Kevin who was the real problem child. After being kicked out of school he started getting into trouble with the police, being brought home by them after being arrested for burglary or nicking cars. He was sent away for stays in youth detention centres. Later, he moved on to other enterprises, but we lived on a council estate and everyone was on the make. I mean, it was a very modern estate, and these days the houses are probably worth over a million, but it was still a South London estate, and if there was trouble my brother would find it. He'd have stolen from his gran if he could. So he'd be in and out of detention centres or sent away to a special boarding school for juvenile delinquents.

I remember it ripping my mother's heart out. She would take me with her to see him in Borstal. I'd make such a big deal about going to visit him, the gay little brother going to see his big brother in prison. I had these early homoerotic fantasies about visiting him and seeing all these boys, but the nearest I got to any fingers was a Kit Kat. I remember it breaking my mum's heart seeing him there, she would be so upset all the way home but would keep it in and be very quiet. My mum never really cried about the big things in life, always the silly things, like not being able to find a shoe . . .

I saw it as Kevin getting all the attention from her. My younger brother Dean was my dad's favourite, so he got all the attention there. I would just have to get it where I could. And I did.

These days I think you'd call it middle-child syndrome – I wouldn't exactly be naughty on purpose but there was always something going on which I could use to cause drama. Growing up where I did, you learned to look after yourself. You had a ranking and you knew how to defend it. My dad loved us, he was very proud of us and if there was trouble with other kids on the estate he would make us go outside onto the street and fight them. I got my feistiness and mouthiness from my mum. But my dad taught us how to fight and how to stand up for ourselves. He taught us how to pick up a brick, or the nearest thing, and whack someone with it. He would never let you back down, he saw that as weakness and would never allow it. I remember the headmaster caning me, Kevin and Dean at school and my dad marching down there, pinning the head against a wall, and having to be held back from beating him up. We would all have been thrown out if my mum hadn't gone and begged them to keep us there. I think she was horrified at the thought of the three of us being stuck at home and her having to look after us 24/7. It was all very dramatic. Everyone on the estate was talking about it for weeks afterwards. But it was clear: my dad could use force to punish his sons, but God forbid anyone else who tried to come near them.

My mum developed breast cancer when I was about seven or eight and, looking back, it really affected me. It was sad and it was awful; even though it was never really mentioned or discussed in front of us, we would hear our parents talking behind closed doors so we knew what was going on. It changed our home life. My mum would be ill, on the sofa under a duvet watching the TV, struggling to keep up appearances, while my dad would be drinking because he couldn't cope with seeing her that way. I just remember thinking that my mum was such a hypochondriac and being annoyed that she was always ill. Perhaps I didn't want to believe it, and so it was easier to blame her. In the end, Dean and I were sent back to Nanny Surman's in Kent. I can't remember if I ever thought she would die or not, but I missed her a lot. Nanny Surman wouldn't touch Kevin so he went to our other grandparents in Farnborough while my mum went into hospital to have the cancer removed, along with half her stomach, and have treatment.

I was always drawn to drama – and insanity – from as young as I can remember. When I was about five or six my mum took me to visit my great-nan in a nursing home on the King's Road. She had dementia and was just totally batshit crazy. She would have half-eaten sandwiches in her handbag and I thought she was absolutely amazing. On the way back from visiting, we'd go into Tiger Tiger, a posh toy shop on the way home, and I'd get a present as a reward for going along to see her. Maybe in a way a connection was made in my head between craziness and rewards.

One particular family friend would come over to the house for birthdays, Christmas and Easter. She was a complete alcoholic and, like most, would go through different stages throughout the night. She would arrive charming and fun, grow to be the life and soul of the party, then pick a fight with someone before being kicked out to sit on the grass by the house throwing empty booze bottles at buses as they drove past. Obviously, I thought she was absolutely brilliant. Like I said, I was drawn to drama and craziness.

I think it was probably after my mum's breast cancer that I really started acting up. To begin with it wasn't anything out of the ordinary – plenty of little kids have an obsession with fire and I would take a match to anything if I could. At first, it was just little fires on the balcony and then I would see what I could set fire to in the house. This culminated in me setting a pair of curtains on fire and nearly burning down the whole place. God, I got a serious beating for that. After that I would start to develop mysterious illnesses. I'd be taken along to the doctor's with every imaginable ailment under the sun, and from about the age of nine and a half through to twelve I spent two years on crutches due to an unexplained problem with my foot. I mean, what child wants to hobble around on crutches for absolutely no reason? Me, apparently. I was so fucking dedicated to my role, we went to the doctor's repeatedly and then were referred to the hospital for X-rays. When they couldn't find anything wrong after several visits they operated on my foot to try and find the source of the problem. Now it seems completely crazy that they couldn't see it was all a pretence . . .?

There were examples of a certain sense of grandeur, too, even from an early age. I hated catching the bus with my mum and refused to stand at the bus stop. When, obviously, this refusal had been ignored and I was forced to board, I'd exclaim at the top of my voice, 'Do we have to sit here with all these filthy people?' My poor mother must have been absolutely mortified. There were other examples of this sense of self-importance too – from the age of about four, I would drag everything I could from the living room onto the balcony of the flat we lived in at the time, build myself a makeshift stage and perform drag shows for the neighbours. I don't remember there being much of an audience – or, in fact, much of an appetite – for my daily shows, but still I'd put them on. I'd fashion myself in whatever I could find and generally make as much commotion as possible from my little DIY stage. It was around this time that I had a little red mini car that I'd been given for my birthday – the type with pedals that you could drive around in. My God, I loved that car so much. I'd take it down to the kerb every morning and leave it in what I considered to be my parking spot, which obviously took up a space for someone who had an actual real car in need of an actual parking spot. But God forbid anyone should try to move it. I'd march up and down the street questioning any witnesses as if there had been a murder, then when I discovered the culprit I'd think nothing of rocking up to their front door and giving them a piece of my mind on car parking etiquette. I can't remember the number of times our bell would go and it would be a neighbour telling my mum I'd been kicking off again. I don't remember it as trying to be naughty, or obnoxious – I just remember feeling as if I didn't always belong there in that house, with those people. A lot of it felt alien to me.

When I hit my early teens I would get cabs back from town and leave them running outside the house, making my mum go out and pay for it. When she'd tell me off for getting taxis I'd just say, 'Well, you want me to be safe, don't you?' That kind of summed up my entire attitude at the time. Again, I say . . . my poor fucking mother.

As well as drama at home, I tended to seek it out at school, too. I went to a little infant school called Falconbrook and loved it. I was in the school talent show there and dressed up as a girl even then. I mimed along to the song 'Long-Haired Lover from Liverpool' wearing my mum's sparkly top and tights. For the Queen's Silver Jubilee in 1977, there was a fancy-dress competition on my street. I dressed up in a purple leotard, silver strappy sandals with a kitten heel, and a blue satin sash, so there went any chances of fitting in. My dad didn't want me to do it. He didn't have a problem with who I was, or with me dressing up, he just didn't want me to make life hard for myself, to get into trouble with the other kids. I didn't even get the first fucking prize for my efforts because the judges thought I was a girl, rather than a boy in drag.

I remember going for the interview for high school, walking around and deciding that this was where I wanted to be. I made a big display of telling the headmistress that I loved reading, that I'd read all of the *Born Free* books, how I was obsessed with Elsa the lion and wanted to visit Africa. I wanted to impress her, and I did. I got in based on that, my brief turn as an angel child. The charade didn't last too long. Fast-forward a few years and I was camp as Christmas with waist-long wet-look permed hair. I wasn't trying to please anyone.

As a camp young thing who had a habit of drawing attention to himself, I needed protection, and so I became friends with the very roughest girls in the school. These girls were like a pack of wolves – the toughest, meanest and scariest kids in class unless you were their mate, and then they defended you like lionesses. My best mate was always in trouble with the police. I remember us sitting outside the headmaster's office having been banned from our French class when we had taken it upon ourselves to send the teacher death threats, as you do. Real letters, signed by us. We wanted her to know who was winding her up. When I was still allowed into the classroom, I became the class clown. I wanted everyone to like me so made the decision that I would be the loudest, funniest one who caused all the trouble, then at least the ones who didn't like me would be scared of me. Pretty simple plan.

This culminated in me attempting to seduce a teacher at the age of fifteen. I was so full-on, but by that point I had been abused by a man at the local youth group – I'll come to that later – and had started going out on the gay scene and to Heaven night club – I'll come to that too – and had spotted my teacher there. I really fancied him. I would stay late in class, linger around the classroom, helping, and I instigated the whole thing. I remember putting the chairs away and kissing him. He was very 'No, no, this can't happen' and asked to speak to me after school. He told me, 'I'm a grown man, you're a child – this cannot happen.' But I had this big-dick energy and I thought I could have whatever I wanted. I threatened that if he didn't do what I wanted I would tell everyone that he had anyway. I used to threaten to disclose that he was gay to everyone. Now I look back, it's crazy that it ever happened. Long story short, he ended up giving me a blow job and as I was leaning against the window, it opened and I fell out and everyone at school saw me with my pants down. My mum was called into school and it was agreed by all that it would be best if I didn't go back, so that was the end of my schooling. My mum thought it wise not to tell my father, for obvious reasons, and so every day I would get dressed in my uniform, leave for school, and hang around on the estate instead, or head down to the King's Road.

And so, expelled from school, I spent most of my time hanging out with the older kids from the estate. Evenings were normally spent hanging out on The Wall, which was, quite literally the wall on the corner on the patch of grass on the estate. But we all used to spend our free time there, the whole gang. There were probably about twenty or thirty of us in total. We did what teenagers do, a bit of underage drinking and some small-time tinkering and thievery. I still hung out with the tough girls from school. Most of them had started to have babies, which were dumped on my mum while we went about the all-consuming business of being teenagers.

We were terrors but in quite an innocent way really, we were never malevolent. (Okay, apart from the death threats.) Admittedly, we built up to stealing cars and breaking shop windows, but there was a general rule that you didn't steal from your own. The only time I ever got into trouble with the police growing up was when I was eleven and managed to cause a ruckus with some local football supporters. God knows what it was about, and I can't even remember what I said, but whatever it was, I'm sure it would have been delivered with full velocity, and whatever came out of my mouth was enough for the police to take me home for my own safety. They thought I was about to be lynched, and I probably was.

One of the ongoing sagas from my childhood was the power struggle for the biggest bedroom. As anyone who's grown up with siblings in a three-bed semi will testify, the struggle is real. For as long as I remember, I'd been trying to get a room of my own, having had to share with Dean for most of our childhood, and there was no fucking way I was sharing with Kevin the Antichrist. In the end, after years of wearing the whole family down with various schemes, tantrums and threats, I was granted sole occupation of the box room. I was delighted, but it was short-lived. Kevin had got into trouble with the police – again – and was sent away to a youth detention centre. Permanently. I'm not sure that concerned me too much, to be honest – the biggest drama as far as I could see was that this meant Dean got the big bedroom all to himself. I was apoplectic. Things were going to have to change. I tried all my normal schemes – tantrums, bribes and general family abuse – but for possibly the first time in my life my mum stuck to her word and didn't fold under my constant pressure. I'd caused so much trouble getting the box room, she said that was where I would have to stay. Somebody – Dean – would have to pay.

I only had to harbour this grudge for about a decade before fate delivered revenge into my hands. Dean, then a young teen, had been up on Clapham Common with mates, and my mum found a bag of E's in his pockets when she was clearing up the floor of our rooms to do the laundry – something she did well into our teens and twenties. When she pointed them out to him he told her they were headache pills, and she popped the bag to one side in the kitchen. He fully planned to grab them as soon as he had the chance but before that, my mum came down with a migraine. 'Dean, I took one of your pills for my head,' she shouted up the stairs. He shat himself and ran out of the house.

In the end, my mum just had to go and lie down but not before she did a turn as a demented show pony. Her eyes were rolling in her head, she was pacing up and down and her mouth was like a typewriter. I dobbed Dean in as fast as I could. My dad was not impressed and swiftly followed him out of the house and collared him in the pub. Later on, when I started going out properly, my mum used to find coke in my pockets and I'd blame it on Boy George. Every time she found a bag of E's, I'd just say that I'd taken them off him because he was too high. My mum and dad absolutely loved George. He used to come round to the house all the time and would be on his best behaviour, like butter wouldn't melt. My dad loved Steve Strange too. He used to come round selling dodgy goods. He lived down the road and would go out with 'found' credit cards, buy a load of electric goods and then bring them round your house for you to buy. Like I said, you didn't steal from your own, but if it had fallen off the back of a lorry then that was absolutely fine.

And that leads us to me bursting fur-clad from the closet, ready for my baptism of fire on one of the most exciting social scenes on the planet.

THINGS I LEARNED FROM SCHOOL

Nothing, I never fucking went.

I learned that I'm not the academic type.

That I was a really great escapologist.

I learned that I had a real talent for drama.

That turning up to your first day at secondary school with
waist-length black tight-curled permed wet-look gelled hair is
not the best way to start.

I learned survival skills. If you ever fear for your safety,
always make friends with the meanest, hardest bitches you
can. No one will mess with you.

I learned where the back door was, where the smoking area
was, and when to avoid people.

I learned to always be the loudest person in the room.

That it's not acceptable to hit someone over the head with a
cricket bat when they bowl you out.

When you're not quite ready to come out, then
it's not the best idea to ask to appear in the
school play in full drag.

That I don't like uniforms.

2.
The King's Road

To this day, Siouxsie Sioux is the only person to have ever had the balls to slap me right across the face. We were in the Limelight Club – me, Boy George and my friend Richard Habberley – and she whacked me full-on, three claws scraping across my face. I was so outraged that I was speechless, and believe me, that rarely happens.

It wasn't unprovoked – but it wasn't the worst stunt I'd ever pulled either. By far. We'd turned up at the club and it was like the night of a thousand fucking Siouxsie Siouxs. Christ, at that time everyone looked like her. The same blackbird's-nest hair, the same make-up – a pencilled-in eyebrow, a red lip and a load of black eyeliner and eyeshadow – and the same clothes . . . everything. I took it upon myself to tell this girl that I was standing next to that she looked like shit and asked why she was such a pathetic try-hard dressing like Siouxsie? I continued to tell her that the real one was fucking terrible and didn't have an ounce of style. Naturally, I hadn't realised she *was* the real Siouxsie, and so there you go – I got slapped. I have a vague memory that Vivienne Westwood nearly punched me on the same night, so I must have been really asking for it.

It was the beginning of the 80s and I was making a name for myself as one of the most obnoxious and arrogant fuckers on the scene. And, whatever you thought of my methods, I was gaining notoriety, and that was something. I can't remember the number of times Boy George or one of my other mates would be taken to one side and told that I was out of control and to have a word with me, but they didn't have any control over me either. I had decided that my USP was to be the loudest, most obnoxious person in the room, so that's what I set about being.

My crew at that time mainly revolved around Boy George, who I'd nicknamed Gina, we'd never fucking call him Boy George, and Richard, and our lives ricocheted between the King's Road and Soho. The King's Road scene at the time was everything, a Mecca for anyone creative or different, and Soho had so many clubs that we had somewhere to go every night of the week. The 80s was an incredible decade to be in London, and it spawned so many amazing people. It was such a creative time and tribe mentality was really coming into play. People were dressing up, New Romanticism was ending and everyone was into Westwood and Gaultier. There was a gang that wore head-to-toe Yohji Yamamoto and a gang that wore Versace. What you wore was everything.

You had to have a look to be seen and to back up that look you had to have a voice and be heard. The difference between now and then is that you had an audience that was real, not virtual. Now, kids might put on a look in their bedroom, take a picture, put it up on Instagram and TikTok and let technology do the rest. They can reach millions of people without even leaving their room while they scroll through to see what their peers are wearing and doing. But the King's Road was our social media – you went there to be seen and everyone would walk up and down the road all day long. It was the Facebook of our time. People would stop you and take photographs of you and it was a hub of activity. On a Saturday it would take you two hours to walk down the road and back, it was so packed.

My own induction to the King's Road was at fifteen when I managed to get a Saturday job at the NHS newsagent's. I was this chavvy, chubby thing with a second-hand Del Boy sheepskin coat and a big mouth. It didn't take long for me to get the measure of things and instigate a dramatic image overhaul. First of all, I worked out you needed clothes, and to get the clothes you needed cash. So I started nicking from the newsagent's. It was a simple set-up – I would put cigarettes out with the rubbish, go back for the bag after closing and then take them around the pubs selling them.

It was at the NHS newsagent's that I met the DJ Tasty Tim – he's a few years older than me and was already very much involved in the King's Road scene. He took me under his wing and introduced me to the Great Gear Market, where I soon ended up getting a job. The Great Gear Market was halfway down the King's Road, where the Marks & Spencer's is now. It was made up of loads of little stalls selling clothes from independent designers. You entered through a shop door and went down some stairs into this big space. I remember meeting Princess Julia there – she's still around on the London scene DJ'ing and still being Princess Julia. Back then she was already a name around London. She had this massive beehive, all matted at the back, with bright make-up and was the most glamorous person I'd ever met. She was known as being one of the faces for the band Visage after she'd been in their 'Fade to Grey' video. I remember her looking me up and down and asking me how old I was; she says she still remembers me wearing a school uniform when we first met. Everyone used to hang out at the Great Gear Market during the day and I joined the crowd. I heard that one of the stands was looking for a Saturday kid, so I went up to them, blagged a load of experience and that was that. I had the job on Diana's stall situated behind the cage – which was Rusty Egan's record shop – selling young designers and one-offs – it was very streetwear. It was there that I met Gina for the first time. This was before he got massive. He came in and the first thing I noticed about him was his dreadlocks, so obviously that's how I decided to start the conversation. 'Who does your hair?' I asked. 'It's shit.' And he was like, 'What did you say, love?' 'You've got shit locks, mate.' That was it. There was no foreplay. I was a chubby little queen with a ton of attitude.

Gina was working as a shop assistant at the Foundry, a shop on Carnaby Street, and I remember going in and he would be like, 'What do you want? Get out the door,' and he'd kick me out. I told him to fuck off, but I had to find a way around it. I hung around with these girls called Julie and Beshenka from Croydon. They were goths, with off-the-shoulder tops and loads and loads of jewellery piled everywhere. They wore flat shoes and would shuffle along like something from *The Ring*. Everything was covered in make-up powder, every collar had a make-up line on it. They had big bright-red backcombed hair and were really thin and Gina was obsessed with them.

They essentially made me look a lot cooler and thinner by association and I decided that they were my best way in. 'You can come in, darlings, but that cunt can fuck off,' he used to say. That's how we became friends, and how our friendship is to this day. We would just argue with one another. I remember going to see one of Culture Club's first gigs on Foubert's Place and being a bit like, 'What's this shit?' But they were fucking amazing, and I'd already decided he was going to be my best mate. I was in total awe. He hated me because I was so snarky to him, but I was persistent, and he's still one of my best friends now.

It was through Gina that I met Richard. We quickly became a little trio of party boys. Richard was one of the most handsome boys in London – it was a bromance right from the start. Richard lived with Gina when I first met him and I was at their flat all the time. Richard was a little style icon – everyone wanted to be Richard, everyone wanted to hang out with Richard. We'd go out every night of the week and rule – he had the best looks and was just so, so much fun. He was one of the first people to wear Day-Glo and was always ahead of his time. When Vivienne Westwood did the Witches Collection, he was one of the first people to wear all that. Richard was from Chigwell, and when he moved to London he found himself really quickly. He was always going to find himself – he was so good-looking. I used to be envious of him because he would get the boys I wanted. He had a model physique, small waist and a V-shaped back and this bleached hair that changed colour like the days of the week. I got Richard a job working on the stand with me at the Great Gear Market and I taught him how to steal. We'd help ourselves to the money from the till and then we'd do stock checks to make sure the numbers added up – on paper at least. In reality, it was a case of sell one, pocket one, and put the money down our socks. At that time the goths were the reigning tribe. They all had pet rats which they would carry around town as part of their look. I'd flick them off their shoulders. If I had to choose a soundtrack to that particular phase of our lives it would be the Sisters of Mercy *First and Last and Always* – we lived our lives to that album.

Our whole lives revolved around the Great Gear Market and we thought we ruled the place. Throughout our time there we had a long-running hatred for a woman called Alison who worked next door at the Review – another clothes shop. She was vile and we loved to taunt her, but she sold Katharine Hamnett, which we wanted. Anyway, she really thought she was it and we fucking hated her. So when we finally left the market, I sent her a funeral wreath and she called the police.

We were obsessed with John Waters films and in particular his film *Female Trouble*, which revolves around a character called Dawn Davenport who leaves home, gets knocked up, has a terror child and embarks on a life of crime. We based ourselves on the character and her morals, which is why we sent the wreath, robbed the shop and threw a brick through a window.

The brick incident came about because I had heard that a backing singer of Gina's who used to come into the Great Gear Market had told the dancer Michael Clark that I was the most hated boy in London. I was fucking livid to the point that I was determined to teach her a lesson. I had no idea if the story was true or not, but we got into the car with Sue Tilley (who was part of our crew at the time and who went on to model for Lucien Freud) driving and headed over to take revenge. I decided to brick her window but when we got there I couldn't find a brick so I ran up and down the road trying to find something to smash the windows with. In the end, I found a rock, launched it at her house, jumped back in the car, and shouted to Sue, 'Fucking Drive!!!' When the backing singer confronted me about it years later, I said I did it to try and make her a better person. Like fuck I did.

Nowadays when it comes to fashion there are so many high street brands that take inspiration from designers that you can wear a cheap version of something and still look great, but back then if you wanted to be on trend you had to wear designer. It was either retro or what was being designed. We didn't have a whole back catalogue of Alexander McQueen to reference back then, so you had to be current, and to do that you had to be able to afford the clothes, which is why we were always on to some con or another.

The scams that we were running weren't exclusive to the Great Gear Market by any extent – they stretched all the way down the King's Road and through to Soho. We would have these boys called hoisters who would come in and you'd give them your shopping list. For example, I'd tell them we wanted the Westwood tracksuit, the Westwood boots, the Katharine Hamnett tee, that we wanted this and we wanted that, and they'd go off and nick it for us, and we'd buy it off them at a knock-off price with the profits we'd nicked from our stand during the day. A load of the stuff I gave to Boy George in the early days was procured by hoisters. Thank God he never knew. We'd leave work on a Saturday night with our ill-gotten gains in our pockets and go down to Jones, buy new clothes and then turn up at work wearing them the next day. People were no fools and would ask us where we managed to get our new designer clobber from. 'Oh, George gave it to me,' was the standard response.

In the end, we got sacked. Of course we did: we were two kids who always had this unexplained cash, wearing expensive clothes all the time. But we managed to keep our little hustle going for a few years before we got turfed out completely. The thing was, I knew everyone and they would come to the shop to see us, so we brought traffic, we brought noise, and we brought excitement to the place, so we got away with murder. But then, like I always do, I pushed it just that little bit too far.

It was only when we got sacked and went on to find our next job that we got into our first proper trouble. Richard Habberley and I went to work for Margi, a prostitute on Cromwell Gardens in West Kensington. I think it might have been in the old East German Embassy. We had heard about the job in one of our regular pubs and thought it would be a laugh. My job was to play receptionist, dressed as Moana the maid. The law at the time said that if two women were both sex workers in the same house, then it was a brothel. A boy in drag manning the reception desk solved the problem. Margi had to be the glamorous one – she had this bleached blonde bob, tiny waist and these huge tits – so I wore a short grey curly wig and an apron dress. It was turquoise with little flowers and stopped just above the knee and was paired with thick tights and a sensible court shoe. I used to sit there putting red lipstick on and Margi would absolutely hate it, shouting, 'Get that shit off your face, Moana. No lipstick!' There were some men who would come and want a man in the room watching them, so I'd have to take Moana off and put a bomber jacket and jeans on and play butch. Oh, it was good fun at Margi's. We used to go out with her too, she really was very glamorous, always in furs and leopard print coats. One night we went out with her and John Galliano – he dressed her in a hessian sack put a belt around the waist and she still looked amazing.

There was one punter who used to come into Margi's who was a crossdresser with a prosthetic leg. He liked to be tied up to the wall wearing a baby-doll dress and a blonde wig and spanked every half an hour. Margi would start him off and then go off to watch EastEnders or Corrie and send me in to carry on. When Margi went in to spank him it would be like 'whack, whack, whack' and then I'd go in and it would be more like 'WHAACK, WHAACK, WHAACK'. He'd totally freak out and lose his shit. I remember one time I was spanking him so hard that the leg came off and got twisted up in his tights. Margi came in and screamed at me to get out of the room. I didn't know how hard I was meant to hit him, did I?

Richard's job was to go around putting flyers in phone boxes while I sat on reception and answered the calls. 'Hello sir, would you like some details of our young lady? Nineteen years of age, she's five foot eight inches tall, 36–22–36, one of the best figures I've ever seen, sir. What service would you require today, sir? We're open until 10pm, sir. Where are you now? Ooh, Earl's Court, we're not far if you jump in a taxi, sir.' It went on like this for about six months until one night we were having an after-party – me, Richard and our friend Lisa – at Margi's house after we'd been to the Lyceum Club and the police kicked the door down, raided the place and arrested everyone.

It was quite a scandal. Margi had sent two guys round to scare her ex-girlfriend – it was a long and ongoing feud after a messy break-up, but it went horribly, horribly wrong. The ex-girlfriend had been found dead – a rubber cosh shoved down her throat. The problem being that it was the same rubber cosh that we used to keep next to the reception desk, and I had a terrible habit of chewing my nails or pens, or anything lying around, and this included the cosh. So I ended up in the Old Bailey giving evidence. I remember the judge saying, 'Would you call yourself a transvestite, Mr Marnoch?' And me replying, 'Sir, I am wearing a Jean Paul Gaultier men's dress and boots with a jacket to match. No, I would not.' I then stepped out of the witness box to give a twirl and show the jury. Tasty Tim was in court giving evidence too, and they were telling us about everyone who'd been up in the Number One court there before us. They were like, 'Myra Hindley was in here you know, Peter Sutcliffe was in there.' The case was pretty serious, not that we thought it at the time. But because we had seen all the comings and goings at Margi's, I was called up to give evidence against three of the accused. 'Mr Marnoch, can you tell me why your teeth marks are in the end of this truncheon?' the judge asked me. 'Oh, you know me, Your Honour, I can't help putting everything in my mouth!' And I held my hands up to the jury and opened my mouth for full effect. I treated the whole thing like a stand-up comedy show but Margi and the two guys ended up going down for murder.

So, exiled from the Great Gear Market and without Margi's to take over, Richard and I had to find a new hangout. Luckily at the time we had these friends called Liz, Maxine, Louise and Debbie who lived in a basement in Cleveland Square, and so after the trial, we'd spend all of our time there instead. We were like parasites . . . I was still supposedly living at home with my mum and dad but would always be round at other people's houses. Whoever had the best flat, we'd go round and install ourselves until we'd ruined it or dined and wined them dry. We would exhaust every resource. Sue Tilley had a landline at her flat in Camden, so we'd head back there after we'd been clubbing, sit on the stairs off our nuts and call all our friends in New York who were just heading out and coming up on their pills. In the end, she was so sick of us she ripped the phone out of the wall and threw it over the balcony. Seemed a little extreme to me, but there you go. Like I said – we were parasites. Anyway, back to Liz's basement flat. Liz used to make all of Boy George's geisha girl clothes; she's now the head of menswear at Ralph Lauren in New York, but back then she and her friends were fashion students and used to run up clothes for us all. We'd always take over their place after a night out and invite everyone back. It wasn't saved for weekends but was standard practice every night of the week and that's where we came up with the idea for what, still now, I think might have been one of my best creations: Diana Dogg.

I had decided to enter the world of cabaret. My friend Robert Perino was running a new night called Trash at the

Camden Palace; he was one of the most flamboyant, in-demand club promoters of the time. He suggested that I do a drag act for his 'Gong Show' he was putting together, where you went on and they banged a gong for you to get off stage if you were shit. They never gonged for me by the way. Diana was my drag act, which was very, very loosely based on Diana Ross. She was a bit of all the Dianas really, Ross, Dors and a little bit of Lady Di. I wore a huge pink bob wig and massive hoop earrings and would trudge around in this great big pink fur coat and fluorescent pink dresses. It was quite a look. I'm over six foot – so six foot six in a wig and heels. No one messes with a big old boy in a chiffon dress.

The Diana Dogg show was an ensemble cast of twelve, made up of a ramshackle crew of my mates on the scene at the time; Princess Julia, Sue Tilley, my friends Polly, Robin, Robbie, Liz, Louise and June, with me as Diana in the starring role. They all had their own little sections and performances and we did entire cast numbers which made up the rest of the show. Our first performance was at the Camden Palace and I performed Diana Ross's single 'Muscles'. I'd nicked a bed from my mum and dad's house and set it up on stage and from there I sprawled, writhed and lip-synced. The show included proper sets and costumes – it was a bit of a shit production put together with sticky tape and cardboard, but it was a production, nonetheless. Sue and Julia would be my backing dancers doing robot-dancing in pillbox hats and Hawaiian grass skirts. Camden Palace soon became our regular venue. When you start doing these things people then ask if you can go and do it at their club too, so we went on tour. I was actually surprisingly good at organising it all and I remember us taking the coach down to Brighton – it was such a gaggle that it was like herding cats and we only just all made it on the bus back. We didn't attempt to tour again after that.

The artist and performer Leigh Bowery made my outfits for Diana Dogg. As for a lot of people, Leigh was a big, big part of the 80s for me. He was such a huge character, both physically and in personality and a real trailblazer on the scene. He pushed the boundaries of performance art and was outrageous. He really was larger than life in every way. I would like to say that there was a crazy story attached to us meeting but we went to the same clubs every night and just ended up becoming friends. I can still remember my favourite outfits that Leigh made for Diana. There was a see-through baby-doll nighty which was hooped and circular at the bottom, with a baby-blue marabou feather trim. I would wear it with a white bra and knickers with a big silver star on the crotch and one on each tit, polka-dot tights, and six-inch heels from She and Me, the old-school trans shop in Olympia. Then there was the great big pink fur coat – which I don't think I took off for about six months – and which I think Philip Salon still wears now. There was a gold sequinned trouser suit that flared out at the bottom with a pink chiffon pussy-bow blouse which I wore under-neath, and a massive matching pink wig. That was a look. I remember shopping for the fabric with Richard in John Lewis – the sequinned fabric was so expensive there was no way we could afford it. In the end, we hoisted the roll up onto our shoulders and walked out backward with it through the tills as if we worked there. Shameless.

It was around then I started doing music for fashion

shows, suggesting the tracks and putting together the soundtrack that would play as the models walked. First I did the music for Katharine Hamnett, and then for Joseph Tricot and Wendy Dagworthy, and then everybody really. It started when I was having dinner with George at St Lorenzo. Robert Forest, who was the editor of *Women's Wear Daily* and is just as fierce now as he was then, was sitting at the table next to us having dinner with the stylist Michael Roberts. He used to come into the Great Gear Market so we started talking and they were telling us that they had a fashion show the next day. Robert went to Michael, 'Ohhh, you gotta get Tony to do the music. Tony's music is gorge, girl!' Those were his exact words and two days later I was doing the show. There I met the fashion PR Lynne Franks who took a shine to me – I think she liked my cockiness – and the next minute I was doing the music for every fashion show in London – and all because of her. Looking back, that was a massive break. It was a big deal for her to take me under her wing. I remember she had this office in Covent Garden with a glass front and this huge desk in the middle. She really did rule London back then and was a force of nature. She would decide you were doing something and before you knew it, you'd be doing it.

Michael and I carried on working together after that and he ended up shooting me as Dusty Springfield for an eight-page piece in *Ritz* – a paper at the time – and then it went into *Tatler* and became the basis for a five-page shoot in *The Face* magazine. The make-up for the *Ritz* shoot was done by Mary Greenwell, who has gone on to be a legend in the make-up industry. It was the early 80s, I was modelling for Joseph in drag, and it was groundbreaking. Everything I wore in the shoot was from the actual collection, including a little Joseph Tricot black shift dress with a white collar, which I've had printed on to hoodies now.

Michael and I had been working with each other on the Joseph London Fashion Week show for three weeks and he was obsessed with Dusty Springfield. Everyone else was playing Diana Ross's 'Chain Reaction' so I said to Michael that I thought we should do something different and make it really camp. It seemed like an obvious solution to bring Dusty into the show and he was like, 'Yeah, let's do it'. So we played Dusty tracks and I dressed up as her for the advertising campaign. The real Dusty tried to sue us because we called it 'The Dusty Springfield Collection' and the main image for the ad campaign was me as Dusty with the male supermodel Paul Sculfor laying naked on a table while I held a knife and fork and pretended to eat his arse. Those pictures were incredible. It was such an amazing time to be in London – there was so much creativity, it was all about talent and a look. If you had that, you were in. It didn't matter where you were from, or whether you were working class or a toff, if you had talent – or a big mouth – you could really be someone.

I was seventeen. London was on fire and it was all to fucking play for.

3.

Lights, Camera, MDMA

Let's set this straight once and for all, shall we? There is only one fucking Freddie Mercury story. It was Saturday night and it was my first time at the nightclub Heaven, which for any gay boy at that time, or even now, was like visiting Mecca. Spoiler: Freddy Mercury gave me my first line of cocaine there. He gave me the gram and told me to go and take it. I went to the toilets and tipped a bit onto my thumb. I don't actually like telling that story too much because I feel like it makes me sound really fucking old, that I was out clubbing even way back then.

I remember walking into Heaven and it was like I was Charlie entering the Chocolate Factory. It was men only on a Saturday night and it was like the doors being opened onto a magic kingdom. There was a little hole-in-the-wall cafe next to the entrance – I must have got there at 10.30 but was too terrified to go in so I hung around there all night drinking cans of Coca-Cola. The people in the cafe and the door guys kept asking me who I was waiting for and I just kept saying I was waiting for my friends. I must have stood there until about 1.30am. I was wearing a white

Fiorucci T-shirt with two angels wings on. Loads of people had chatted to me as they'd gone in but there was one group of guys who walked past and stood smoking outside before they went in. One of them said, 'Nice T-shirt,' and asked why I was waiting there. The doorman shouted over and said I'd been waiting there all night and so they asked if I wanted to go in with them. There were six of them and one of them happened to be Freddie Mercury – it's as simple as that. I wasn't a Queen fan so I didn't know who he was. I was into Soft Cell and stuff like that. We went to the Star Bar, which was this big room upstairs with candles every-where, it had wooden steps up the side of the room covered in cushions and so we sat there and I hung out with them. There was this guy called Bruce who was with them who I messed around with a bit all night and I remember them doing poppers and me being like, 'Urgh, I'm not doing that.'

At the end of the night, they said, 'What are you doing now?' and we all went back to Freddie's place in Holland Park. They had this old kind of silver Victorian serving tray that they were snorting coke off. That night was the first time I had done coke and it was awful. It blocked my nose up and made me feel paranoid. Right from the start. I hated it. I probably didn't do more than one or two lines but I swore I would never do it again. I remember there came a point when all six guys were on the bed and started messing around, but I was so green and nervous that I didn't get involved. I just sat there on the edge of the bed. No one put a finger on me. Or in me. Or anything else. Would make for a better fucking story if they had.

I saw Freddie again at Fashion Aid at the Royal Albert Hall in 1985 when I had to go and get Gina from his house when he was off his nut. It was the fashion version of Live Aid and Gina was modelling for BodyMap. I remember him still being so off his nut while this girl was gluing his hair in. Everyone was smoking smack at the time. Heroin came in waves in London, it came in the late 70s and early 80s and then back again around the late 80s, around the time of Taboo. I never touched heroin but it really was a thing and everyone was doing it. It had London by the balls and in a way it was so acceptable. One well-known designer put heroin in my boyfriend's tea without him knowing. It was fucking outrageous. I went mental when I found out.

Heaven wasn't my first club experience, but up until that point, I'd really just been hanging out with the crew from the Great Gear Market. Everyone used to go from the Great Gear Market to the Chelsea Potter pub and then we'd all go clubbing from there. It was the same as it is now – you go out for a drink after work and then you're a bit like, 'Where shall we go now?' And we'd end up clubbing. We would go to Busby's on a Monday night, which was the first gay club, and then Cha Cha's at the back of Heaven on a Tuesday, Thursday night was Camden Palace, and so on – you could go out every night of the week if you wanted to and every night would be fucking rammed. It was at Cha Cha's that I first met Leigh Bowery and the stylist and designer Judy Blame. I remember Judy had his hair up and tied around some old chicken bone – he looked like something out of the fucking Flintstones. Busby's was just behind Tottenham Court Road, you went in and there was a chrome balcony that ran all around so that you could look down on the dance floor. I loved it there. It felt really glamorous to my teenage mind. It was next door to the Astoria, where

Ghetto used to be and also Substation and Stallions, which was the big gay bar that had porn booths and sawdust on the floor.

We still spent a lot of time partying at our friends Louise, Maxine, Debbie and Liz's basement flat around that time. I remember one night there was this cute rockabilly boy there called Mario and everyone fancied him. He had this girl-friend called Anna who was really fucking annoying and my friend Paul couldn't stand her – we were jealous vicious queens at the end of the day. Anyway, she came up to me in the kitchen one night crying because Paul had been horrible to her. I was off my nut and was giving her a hug when – and I swear I didn't know that Paul was going to do this – he came up behind her with a pair of scissors and cut off her ponytail. I was like, *Oh. My. Fucking. God.* Her hair had been down to the middle of her back and he had cut it into a tiny little bob. After that she was crying hyster-ically and then Mario started kicking off and it just turned into a bit of a brawl.

I mean, it was the 80s in London, man. There were so, so, many stories – we were young, taking the piss out of everything.

My first clubbing experience though was at the Embassy Club. I'd met this guy Roy cruising at the meat rack in Piccadilly and he was the manager there. Roy was this leather queen, and I really idolised him, and he was so, so, sexy. We were never boyfriends but I hung out with him for a while and I was so impressed by his job at the club. The first time I walked in I remember just thinking, *This is it, I've arrived, I love this feeling.* I loved the fact that I could be somewhere and be who I wanted to be without having to give an explanation, without having to have a green light from the people I was with. It was the first time I found real freedom within music, too. I didn't have to pretend, and that was the beauty of it. I remember I had gone to see my friend Ronda to tell her that I was going to the Embassy Club that night and ask her what I should wear. I wore a little blue Puma V-neck with jeans. I was just a young chavvy kid, man. I was sat there and Roy was introducing me to loads and loads of people. I remember waiting for him to finish his shift and sitting in the club in total awe. The Embassy was the biggest club at the time, it was kind of London's answer to Studio 54 – it was camp, it was hyper-sexed, and it was the place to be. There were huge disco balls hanging from the ceiling, the lighting was all neon, and there was a sunken dance floor with a lot of dancing, they were still playing the end of disco when I went there. I remember thinking, *This is where I need to be in life. This is it. I've died and gone to heaven.*

At this point in time I was completely obsessed with Roy. As far as I could see, he was everything a gay man should be. He was really hot, and he was my first major crush. He was the one that gave me poppers, he was the first person I ever had full sex with and I remember standing at the bus stop afterwards thinking, *Fucking hell. I can't believe I did that. I'm a fully fledged gay now.* I saw him on and off for years, but it was just sex – that's gay culture. You have to remember that I was a seventeen-year-old teenager who had the highest sex drive ever. Partly due to hormones and partly because I'd been sexualised at such an early age – I'll get to that later. You know, it was like I'd been given a vocation. I was still living at home in Battersea at this stage, which was really fucking convenient. I got away with doing whatever I wanted to do and it was just down the road from the West End. I remember smuggling boys back all the time. My mum and dad would be next door in their room and I'd be in mine pretending that I was on my own.

My first DJ gig came about because I was doing the door of a night called Playground at the Lyceum Ballroom around this time. It was Rusty Egan and Steve Strange's new night – I knew them from the Great Gear Market and they got me the gig doing the door. Me being me, it wasn't enough. I kept going up to them and telling them that the music was shit and saying that people were walking out because it was so crap and they were telling me how bad it was on their way out. They were like, 'If you think you can do any better then, you do it.' The next week I turned up with four records and that was that, the rest is history. I've never worked another day in my life.

The New Romantic scene and the Blitz scene (which arguably kick-started the entire 80s in London and the club scene as we know it), had made everyone believe that they could open and run their own club nights, so this guy called Chris Sullivan rebranded the Whisky a Go-Go in Soho into the Wag Club, which at that time really felt like a seven-night-a-week super club.

I had decided that DJ'ing was my full-time job now. So, I started at the Lyceum, then I went to the Wag, then to Limelight. Me and Steven Linnard got the gig at Wag first off and started Total Fashion Victim on a Tuesday night and then, the cuckoo that I am, I started DJ'ing on Saturdays and then took it over and turned it into Fattitude and Attitude at the Wag, FAT at the Wag, FAT Saturdays . . . all variations on a theme, and that was that.

After I did that first gig with four records, I kind of built up my record collection instantaneously. The first record I ever bought was The Crusaders' 'Street Life' on twelve-inch, which I went to Clapham Junction to buy. I was back at the Lyceum the following week and then I started doing Tuesday nights, and you know my friends had loads of records so I would borrow theirs and then I would buy more every week, so it didn't take me very long to build up a collection. My older brother had collected records for years and I didn't think twice about helping myself to them. I was going around telling people I was a DJ so they started bringing me records. Before he was a DJ, Paul Oakenfold was an A&R man and he would bring down a brown envelope of records for me at the Wag Club every week. But then we'd go off somewhere else and so I'd ditch them in the bin at the end of the street. I remember someone coming up to me and saying that they'd found a pack of records with my name on in at the end of Wardour Street. I was like, 'Oh my God, I've no idea who put them there . . . thank you!' I dumped them because otherwise I would have to carry them around everywhere all night.

The Wag Club was the first club to get a 6am licence in central London. Prior to that you would go out and everywhere would close at 2 or 3am. Everyone wanted to carry on drinking so there were about six illegal drinking dens in Soho. The Pink Panther was the gay one and it was on Wardour Street above the St Moritz club. It was a door and you went up some stairs and there was a little hole in the door which you'd look through and then they'd let you in. Anyway, we'd all leave the club or whatever bar we'd been at and be like, 'Oh, I'll meet you at Panther's.' There would be me, Leigh Bowery, Trojan, Michael Clark, Princess Julia and loads of Piccadilly rent boys as regulars. It got raided every single fucking night, so we'd all leave, trudge around the block in Soho, wait for the police to go and then we'd go back. We'd all just end up being there until the next day and then stagger out into the daylight to do whatever we needed to do that day.

The Pink Panther really came into its own one Christmas – I think it was 1984. Me, Leigh Bowery and Sue Tilley had spent Christmas Day together at Sue's flat in Camden. Christmas back then meant that everything, and I mean everything, was shut on Christmas Day, even the dodgy off-licence. Anyway, we'd been drinking all day at Sue's and had run out of booze so I came up with the pretty genius suggestion that we raid the Pink Panther for more. We knew the owners well enough to know the booze was kept in a lock-up downstairs but not well enough to feel guilty about robbing them on Christmas Day. It was an illegal drinking club, they were used to not playing by the rules – it wasn't like we were nicking it from a proper boozer, not that it would have made much difference.

So we all got into Sue's car (I'm pretty sure it was some kind of Volkswagen) and drove down into Soho. Leigh had these massive wooden platforms on so he booted the door in, and the two of us ran in and grabbed a load of vodka and crates of beer, while Sue, as ever, waited outside as the getaway driver. We threw it all in the boot, jumped in and just shouted 'Drrrrrriive!' Again, Sue was another long-suffering counterpart in our schemes.

The opening of Limelight changed everything in London. It was the first time London had seen that kind of big New

York-style clubbing production or anything on that level. Even the Wag Club was pretty DIY. Peter Gatien and Don Mclean, who ran the original Limelight in New York, said that they were opening a new club in London and I said, 'Well, obviously you need me to work there for it to be a success otherwise no one will come.' I mean, it was kind of true at the time. I was contracted to be there three nights a week. I'd be there on a Monday, Tuesday and Wednesday, and then at the Wag the rest of the week. The VIP room at the Limelight saw a lot of big celebs. The Limelight in New York was a fucking huge deal at the time so a lot of the big American names would come when they were in town. It was in the VIP room that I first met Nile Rodgers. It wasn't my job to run it but because I was the face of Limelight I'd end up partying with these stars who were visiting out of the goodness of my heart. You know, Nile and I ended up at so many illegal after-hours clubs until late morning.

At that time it was all about clubbing and being seen out and about and I was doing two of the biggest clubs in London – my ego was out of control. I was earning about £7,000 a week, which would be about £20,000 in today's money. It was so much cash for a kid to have. We'd have queues of about 400 people trying to get in. Everyone wanted to come to the Wag and Paul Lonergan would be doing the door. He was one of my closest friends throughout that entire decade. We'd met at the Great Gear Market and were always in trouble but we had such a fucking laugh. Not many people have the magic that Paul had. When he walked into a room, it lit up – he had presence and when you met him you just thought, 'Fuck, this guy's amazing!' Although he lit up the room, he could also turn the lights off with just one line.

There was no rhyme or reason as to how we ran the door at the Wag. One week I'd tell my friend that so-and-so wasn't coming in and they were barred and then the next week when I saw them telling them they couldn't come in I'd be like, 'What are you doing? God, you're so out of order! Of course they can come in.' It was all just about making sure everyone was slightly on the back foot. Some nights there wouldn't be a proper guest list and it would be complete carnage, people turning up and saying that they were my friends and I'd put them on the list, but then of course I would be nowhere to be seen and be staying away from the door or any problems I'd created. A couple of times we decided that we wouldn't let guys under a certain height in, unless they were really, really fit.

At the Wag as you were standing in the queue waiting to go in you could see people go up and down the stairs – often people would be pleading on the door to come in and would ask me to go and talk to Fat Tony. I'd walk up one flight of stairs and then come back down and they'd be like, 'You didn't go and talk to Tony.' At which stage I'd say, 'I am Fat Tony, and you're not coming in so fuck off!' I'd lost a lot of weight since the early days when I'd been given the nickname by Leigh Bowery and Judy Blame – I'd discovered drugs – so at this stage I wasn't quite as easy to spot. There was a curtain that we rolled down which said 'Welcome to the WAG' on it and we'd just be behind it doing coke. Or sticking our heads out from behind it and shouting 'Noo! You can't come in. You're too fat!'

I had to put on a party every week at Limelight and they were insane. One of the first ones I did was 'Fat Tony invites you to blow your top', which was carnival-themed and had a whistle attached to the invite. On another night I filled the club with a giant bouncy castle, and then another time filled it with thousands of polystyrene balls so you could dive into the main dance floor. Limelight was in the old neo-gothic church which is on the corner of Shaftesbury Avenue and Charing Cross Road, just behind China Town in Soho. For months afterwards you'd walk down Shaftesbury Avenue and you would still see these polystyrene balls. I was nineteen and all of a sudden I was running two of the hottest clubs in London. We had queues going all the way down to Leicester Square of people desperate to get into our night and I was flouncing around there in head-to-toe Gaultier – oh, I was a cunt. But I was a funny cunt. I'd come from the estate to doing that and that kind of power goes to your head quite quickly, and then if you introduce drugs into the mix, of course you're going to be a total piece of work. Anyway, whoever was in my company had a fucking great time – yes, sometimes it came at other people's expense but that didn't matter to me back then.

MDMA was a game-changer for us on the scene and Ecstasy came into play at this point. Before that, heroin had a real grip on London, but I never did it. I had a real thing about being on the expensive drugs and it just didn't really appeal to me. I didn't like the effect it had on people – they'd be sat around me just nodding off – I was into uppers. I never injected drugs either, I've always snorted and smoked or shoved stuff up my bum. I couldn't think of anything worse than putting a needle in my arm.

Anyway, Ecstasy came onto the scene and changed everything. There was a guy called Patsy who used to be our dealer in London. He actually turned out to be very good at designing accessories, but at the beginning, we all knew him because he could get his hands on MDMA. This was 1983 and you could only get it in New York then, so he used to bring it back hidden in the shoulder pads of his Jean Paul Gaultier coat. There would be these little black and red capsules that we'd take it in. I remember just thinking. *Oh my God, I love this drug*, and we went on for about four days.

Poor old Pats was a victim of a fair bit of trolling from us. We're friends now, but at the time I thought he was one of the most annoying people to ever walk the planet. Everyone loved him just because he was nice, and I really couldn't get my head around that concept and it fucked me off no end. He kept trying to be mates with Gina, which didn't please me either. He wrote a letter to Gina saying how much he admired him and generally being a bit arse-licky. I wasn't impressed, anyway, so I stole the letter, blew it up and had it printed onto T-shirts, which I gave out in clubs. That wasn't the worst of it either. There was one night in Dodo's and I remember Patsy was wearing a Vivienne Westwood coat from the Witches Collection, I went and cuddled him and whilst I did it I poured poppers down the back of the coat and Paul Lolligan came up behind him and set fire to it just as I let go. We were vile, vile queens. I could go into a room, start on one person, make them cry, move onto the next and not stop until I'd made the whole room cry, and only then would I be satisfied. I saw Patsy years later after I'd got into recovery and was at the stage where you have to try and make amends for everything you've done. I went up to him and started to apologise for trying to set him on fire. He said that hadn't really bothered him but me printing the letter onto the T-shirts had really upset him at the time . . . I was like, *Oh, shit. I'd forgotten about that.*

It was 1985 at the Wag Club where I had perhaps my most famous falling-out of the decade. The front page of the *Sun* newspaper ran the following headline: 'Wham star George Michael was dumped on his backside in a furious fight with a transgender DJ'.

You see, we were all mates but we hated the fact that George Michael was still in the closet and so used to take the piss out of him about it mercilessly. There was a girl called Pat who had been a Boy George fan and then jumped ship and was now in the George Michael camp. I was playing Wham's 'I'm Your Man' and singing over the top of it: 'Call her Fat, call her Pat, call her anything you want because you know she'll sleep with anyone in the Top 40. Pat's George's Beard.' You had to climb up to the DJ Booth in the Wag Club and so George had come up screaming at me to shut up and I pushed him out and onto the dance floor below. I think it was my George (Boy) who then called the *Sun* and leaked the story to them. I was quoted as saying, 'I was only having fun.' George M and I didn't speak for years after that, because it was the beginning of him being outed and the story just got worse and worse in the papers.

We weren't content with ruling the roost in London though. I might have still been living in my mum and dad's box room, but it was the 80s, we were having the time of our lives and we were on a mission for world fucking domination. Boyfriends weren't a thing. Fun was. Gina was one of the biggest pop stars in the world and we'd catch flights like black cabs. The thing with him was, he had more looks than a Grattan's catalogue. All big blousy numbers that would change all the time, so you couldn't keep up. The things that always stayed the same were these massive painted-on eyebrows. They came before him and they were the first thing you saw when he shoved his head out of a cab. Followed by a fucking massive head of dreadlocks, which changed colour every week.

I remember I was on Wardour Street outside the Wag Club and this cab pulls up and the eyebrows come out of a cab window followed by the dreads; 'OI, FATTIMA!' (Which was what George used to call me.) 'I've got to go to New York. You coming?'

'Course I am, Gina, you cunt.'

4.
Ny-lon Life

I remember sitting in the back of a limo on the way to Manhattan from JFK with Steve Rubell, the co-founder of Studio 54, and he said to me, 'Tony! Today you're big news but tomorrow, no one is going to give a fucking shit about you. That's New York.' For emphasis he was taking a massive bump of coke at the time. He must have said that every time he saw me after that. I was a bit like, *Is that the only line you know?* And he'd always reply, in his thick, gravelly Brooklyn accent: 'It's just what you need to know.' Obviously, I was like, 'Fuck off, you cunt, I'm going to prove you wrong.'

The first time I flew to New York was on Concorde for my eighteenth birthday. I must have badgered Gina daily for about a month to get me on that fucking flight. I'd always been a master of manipulating my birthday and never more so than for a big-ticket event like my eighteenth. Everyone was going on Concorde, it was one of the most exciting things to do at that time. Growing up as a kid and having seen the first Concorde flight take off on the BBC news it was really something to aim for. Gina told me to fuck off the first time I asked, but after nagging him every time I could, he finally sorted it out overnight. I caught it on my own and he came out a week later. Before that I'd only ever travelled as far as Spain on a two-week family sojourn in the sun. The glamour of it.

Thing about Concorde, though, once you were on there, it was kind of like being on a coach. It was really small and long and narrow. It was all one class, so you're all on this four-seater all the way down, two one side, two the other. I mean, it wasn't cramped, but I'm not sure it fulfilled my eighteen-year-old brain's fantasy and it definitely wasn't what I'd envisaged. Believe it or not, I didn't even get drunk on the plane. In typical style, even though I wasn't overly impressed by the seating arrangement, I was kind of just wowed by the fact that I was on Concorde. Yes, I'd been hoping for some supersonic boom when we took off and that we'd kind of go into outer space, but even without that, it was still pretty major.

I wasn't the slightest bit nervous about going out to New York on my own. Everyone from my normal gang was there already – the people that I had met on the King's Road, or in Kensington Market and in clubs like Taboo or Cha Cha's. People like Jeffrey Hinton, who was a DJ and part of the scene at the time, and Trojan, who was very much pivotal to the club scene at the time and Leigh Bowery's right-hand man. All of that lot were there doing a show for BodyMap, which was one of the buzziest labels on the planet at the time – it really did sum up the moment, lots of print, lots of jersey and very graphic. The gang and BodyMap going over to New York really was like a Brit-fucking-pop take-over. People from England were the biggest stars on the planet. Andy Warhol and all of that crew were still around in New York then, but still, if you were British, everyone wanted you, which was why we were being flown over to DJ and do fashion shows. Sade was there, the hairdresser Sam McKnight, and all the models had moved there and were working. It was the most happening place on the planet but they looked at our tiny little bubble, thought London was buzzing, and wanted a part of it. Everything felt exciting in New York to be honest – Dunkin' Donuts was exciting, buying Tropicana orange juice was exciting. You couldn't get any of that stuff in England. The first thing I'd do when I got off the plane was go and get a carton of orange juice.

You couldn't really compare the two cities. The energy of New York was completely different to London, and London was tiny in comparison. The West End scene in London was the size of a postage stamp – you could walk from one side of the West End to the other in ten minutes flat. You had the Wag Club, which was the epicentre of it all in Soho. West London had the 325 which was on Euston Road, then the predominantly black drinking clubs like People's and All Nations – which were on Edgware Road towards Maida Vale. The clubs were in the West End, though – there was nothing happening outside of that.

In New York I don't remember ever needing ID to go into clubs or bars, there was no one checking that you were over twenty-one. But New York was very different back then, it was mad. You had all the transexual hookers in the Meatpacking District, and there were places like Avenues A, B, C and D – known as Alphabet City – which were no-go areas to some, but which were home to The World and Save the Robots clubs. Walking back from there on a really hot night there would be people sitting on the street selling clothes and shoes – whatever they could get their hands on really.

You would go to New York and they would have these completely insane club spaces. The most insane was the Hippodrome, which was like hi-tech trash. To walk into Area on Hudson Street with its floor-to-ceiling windows would completely blow your mind. When you walked in you passed a row of windows, like shop windows, and it was just crazy in comparison to anything we had in London at the time. In the windows you had actors dressed up – they had an Alice in Wonderland theme with a guy dressed as a caterpillar sitting on a mushroom smoking a shisha pipe, then you'd go through to another room and there would be people swimming in a fake sea – and that was just on the way into the club. They had an Elvis one time and a road trip theme where they turned the entire middle of the club into a trailer trash park with caravans.

Compared with, say, the Hippodrome in London, which was total trash with terrible cheap light displays, New York was like a different world. You would walk into the Palladium and it was like everything you'd ever heard about Studio 54, and you'd never been anywhere like it in your life. You went in via this old disused cinema entrance that looked like it was completely derelict and then through into this huge hallway with 100ft columns of white silk billowing and then into the main auditorium. There were other bits of the club – like the Kenny Scharf room, which was all spray-painted telephone boxes – and then rooms created by different artists – like the Mike Todd room on the top floor. It was just mind-blowing – you went in and it had massive rafters which had strips of parachute silk draped all over them and fans blowing them, then they had hundreds and hundreds of candles – it was almost like the VIP room without saying it, the Mike Todd room was the place to be. There were clubs within clubs within clubs. There was nothing to even compare it to in London.

I was never star-struck in New York because I felt that I was with the biggest stars on the planet, being there with Boy George and the London crew. When I met Diana Ross I think that was the most star-struck I've ever been. She came over to us and we ended up going to Paradise Garage with her. George had been appearing at the Apollo for a Motown party with Stevie Wonder, so they were all there, which is how we met her and everyone from that planet. That level of stardom was kind of insane. It was like going to the biggest fucking firework display I'd ever seen – just the size and the intensity of it all – the stars, the clubs, the scene – was a drug in itself.

The first time I met Andy Warhol was when he came to Total Fashion Victim, which was a club night in London, then when I was in New York doing the after-parties for Sade's tour, Warhol would come down and it kind of felt like he was always just there. He'd take Polaroids of us. I've still got two Polaroids he took somewhere. There's one of me and Sade, and one of me and George where I'm wearing a big Yohji black polka-dot skirt. But really we didn't care that he was Andy Warhol, we didn't really care about a lot of things to be honest. He could have been Andy, Mandy or Sandy, we didn't give a fuck.

I met the artist Keith Haring when he first came to hang

out in London. He was part of the Wild Bunch – Neneh Cherry and all of the Buffalo Crew, her husband Cameron, the producer Nellee Hooper and Ray Petri, who created the buffalo look and had put Nick Kamen on the cover of *The Face* in a skirt. Keith did the print design for Vivienne's Witches Collection in 1983, and I met him when he came over to do that. We just got on really well – he loved a night out and was hilarious, he was quick-witted and sharp and could keep up with me, which at the time was a rarity. I would DJ at Jungle and Cafe de Paris and we just started hanging out. We'd go off to an after-hours and then when I started doing this club in Paris every Wednesday night, he would come with me – we'd just go over for the night, go out and come straight back to work in London the next night at Cafe De Paris. I was taking drugs at that stage but I wasn't an addict. I was just taking what I needed to get the job done, a few lines to keep me going. I was the party guy at the end of the day.

The drugs in New York were next fucking level. For a start the dealer would come to your house with a briefcase, and you could get an 'eight ball', which we hadn't even heard of in England then – it's an eighth of an ounce of coke, and it would come as a rock in a little bag. I remember the first time I saw one and it might as well have been the Star of Africa diamond. After I'd got over that I was like 'Bags! Wow! They've got bags!' In London you could get your coke in these tiny little wraps of paper – you'd be getting it in last week's *TV Times*. The difference in quality was insane – a tiny little bit of an eight-ball would freeze your face off, it was mind-blowing. Our New York dealer was amazing, he was this Puerto Rican guy called Choo

Butter wouldn't melt!

Me and Mum

Dad

Me on the right with my brothers

Aged 14 at The Wag with
Richard Habberly

Miss Dunston aged 12

First DJ residency at The Jungle 1985

Gossiping with Leigh Bowery at Jungle

At The Wag

With Vaughn Toulouse

Davina McCall

Me & George raving in Ibiza

With Eric Holah at Taboo

Fat Tony: Bigmouth strikes again

DJ of the month in I-D

With Barry Kamen

With Leigh Bowery

Andy Warhol & Keith Haring

Behind the scenes of some 80s pop star video with Gerlinde, Trojan, Polly etc

With Keith, Gil Vazques & Barnsley

JUNGLE
the game

mondays at 157 charing x rd
from june 17
£1 before 11
£2 before 12
£3 after 12
10 to 3
the hunter
gets captured by
£3 drugs ?

...day, men and women
and their friends

Mondays at
157 Charing Cross Road

10.30pm – 3.30am

£2.00 before 11pm
£3.00 before 12pm
£3.50 afterwards

JUNGLE

The Playground
Every Saturday

28 JAN 1985

Steve Strange + Rusty Egan with Klein Müzix

Admit one FREE of CHARGE before midnight on a bribe

Wellington Street W.C.2 10–3 a.m.
admission with invitation only
management reserve the right of admission

LEIGH BOWERY & FAT TONY
Present

1985   1986

Cabaret
PICCADILLY

PRICE £7.00   DENMAN ST.
LONDON W1.

PERFORMANCE
COMMENCES
NEW YEARS EVE
10.45

Heaven
Nothing Like It...
Never Will Be!

LIMELIGHT
LONDON · NEW YORK · CHICAGO
A COMPLIMENTARY DRINK

WAR.

FAT TONY'S 21st BIRTHDAY

LIMELIGHT
LONDON · NEW YORK · CHICAGO

FAT TONY WEIGHS IN

Bank Holiday Monday,
4th May 1987

On 4th May b
2 shows befor
and a very s

THE FACE
AT LIMELIGHT
136 SHAFTESBURY AVENUE WC2

10:30PM–3:00AM
MONDAY JULY–21

DJS JAY STRONGMAN, VAUGHN
TOULOUSE, FAT TONY

THIS TICKET ADMITS ONE

LIMELIGHT

LIMELIGHT
LONDON · NEW YORK · CHICAGO

FAT TONY INVITES YOU TO BLOW YOUR TOP

WE ARE 1
Join Us For Our
FIRST BIRTHDAY

PARTY

Monday 13th July
1987

LIMELIGHT
136 Shaftesbury Avenue

With The Best Sounds Of
The First Year By:
FAT TONY
JEFFREY HINTON
JAY STRONGMAN
BOILERHOUSE
DAVE DORRELL
JEREMY HEALEY

Doors Open 9:30 p.m.

Complimentary Birthday
Cocktails Until 10:30 p.m.

Birthday Cake, Ice Cream &
Jelly at Midnight

This Pass Admits You
& A Party Animal

TWO *perverts* BALLS *in* ONE!
(*up & down*)

THE STRAIGHT CHRISTMAS *bender*!
with the dinner

VAUGHN TOULOUSE *and* FAT TONY
+ big guest surprise

HEAVEN
Underneath The Arches Charing X Way
THURSDAY 11 December

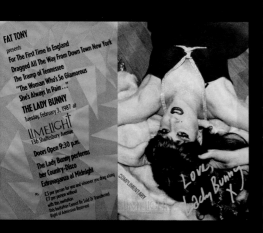

FAT TONY

presents
For The First Time In England
Dragged All The Way From Down Town New York
The Tramp of Tennessee
"The Woman Who's So Glamorous
She's Always In Pain..."
THE LADY BUNNY
Tuesday, February 3, 1987 at

LIMELIGHT
136 Shaftesbury Avenue

Doors Open 9:30 p.m.

The Lady Bunny performs
her Country-Disco
Extravaganza at Midnight

£5 per person for you and whoever you drag along
£7 per person without
with this invitation
This Invitation Cannot Be Sold Or Transferred
Right of Admission Reserved

Love,
Lady Bunny X

Fat Tony
invites you to

Spunk

at

LIMELIGHT

Thursday, July 24th
9 p.m. to 3 a.m.
136 Shaftesbury Avenue
★
Star Turns at Midnight
★
£5 per person with this invitation
£7 per person without

This Invitation Not Transferable
Right Of Admission Reserved

A R E A

Complimentary Drink

MICHAEL TODD ROOM

DOORS OPEN 11PM
OPEN BAR 11PM TO 1AM

MICHAEL TODD ROOM
123 EAST 13 STREET NYC 212.473.7171

COMPLIMENTARY ADMISSION FOR TWO
THIS INVITATION CANNOT BE
SOLD OR TRANSFERRED

PALLADIUM

AT WAG CLUB
total, total, total,
FASHION VICTIMS

WARDOUR ST. W.1.
10:30 - 4:00

Fat Tony & London's Finest D.J.'s

Every Sat.

FATITUDE

at the Wag.

WAG CLUB·35 WARDOUR ST. W1.

FAT TONY
invites you to

*if you aint dreamin'
you've got to be a*

Screamin'

BOY's birthday
@ GET HAPPY!
June 14th 1988

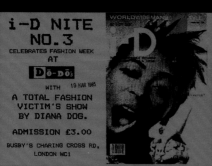

i-D NITE NO. 3

CELEBRATES FASHION WEEK
AT

Dō-Dōs

WITH 19 MAR 1985

A TOTAL FASHION
VICTIM'S SHOW
BY DIANA DOG.

ADMISSION £3.00

BUSBY'S CHARING CROSS RD,
LONDON WC1

WORLDWIDE MANIA

Wag CLUB

EVERY FRIDAY
10PM - 4AM

"SPIRITUALLY
GROOVY!"

DJ's
ANDY
WEATHERALL
FAT
TONY
PAUL
OAKENFOLD
JOHNNY
WALKER
+
GUEST P.A.

ADMISSION £30-

LIMELIGHT
071 434 0572

When Diana Dogg ruled the world!

The Sixties Show at DoDo's

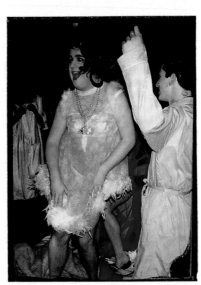

The Love Show at Cha-Cha's

Diana Dogg & Tasty Tim getting married at Heaven

Leigh as high priest!

With Richard Habberly & Polly

At Cha-Cha's with Alice 1983

Wearing Leigh's babydoll dress

The Disco Show with Sue Tilley

The Hawaiian Show with Princess Julia at Camden Palace

Diana Dogg & Sue Tilley in The Face Magazine 1985

Catwalk as theatre. Under the direction of Michael Roberts, the JOSEPH TRICOT shows for London Fashion Week have become one of the hottest tickets in town. Last season Roberts' *coup de theatre* was a swarm of Tina Turner clones. This year Club DJ "Fat" Tony Marnoch dragged up as Dusty Springfield to a backing track of "You Don't Have To Say You Love Me". The mini-skirted male models, hobbling on stiletto heels, were appreciably more bashful. Shows, p64-69

I-D Magazine 1986

Weeping Dusty Springfield's for JOSEPH TRICOT. The male models didn't want to but Fat Tony forced them.

Choo who would come around, and he had his little brief-case which he'd open and it would have bags of mushrooms hanging up along the top, big fat Mexican mushrooms, and then speed balls, coke and MDMA, and you'd say, 'I'll have this, this, that and that.' You'd just page him and he'd be there in ten minutes. It was a party boy's dream.

My uniform at the time was Yohji and Gaultier. When I met the Beastie Boys and started hanging around with Adam Yauch from the band and the rest of the boys, all of a sudden I was hip-hop Tony – I'd wear tracksuits and I had these gold necklaces made with 'Puff' and 'Queen' on them from those hip-hop shops on Canal. I first met the Beastie Boys at Palladium and then they came to London to hang out. I was running Limelight at that point – they'd call up and ask what we were doing so I'd get them down to my night. I met them through Keith Haring, who was like, 'You've got to meet these boys, they're really cute.' And that's how we started. I remember being out with them on a Tuesday night in New York. We'd been in this shitty club on 14th Street and then we went to a house party. They were just lunatics but obviously I thrived off that. And they were cute lunatics too, which helped. I remember being there and they were smoking spliffs and playing pool and I just thought it was really boring, but then it just totally kicked off and they started smashing everything up. I would thrive on that stuff and just get more mental – anything they were doing I would just have to do louder and better. I was a total chameleon. I would be out with them and they just did whatever they wanted to do and were riding a wave. They were notorious for being wild and I fucking loved it.

I was back and forth every other week after that, so at that point in time I went over and stayed in Charles Atlas's house with Jeffrey Hinton, Trojan – who was Leigh Bowery's best friend – and John Maybury, so that was when I really got to know everyone. Then Gina came over a week later with Richard Habberley, Alice Temple and Jane Goldman – who's now married to Jonathan Ross – and they were all at 88th and Columbus, so obviously I decided I was going to move into Gina's house. And then we started going clubbing. Michael Clark was there, the make-up artist Lesley Chilkes, David Holah and Stevie Stewart from BodyMap. I met Steve Rubell with Gina so he was like, 'You should come over and do Total Fashion Victim for us,' so within a month they were flying us out to do Total Fashion Victim, and that's where it all just snowballed from.

I remember us going to a Yohji Yamamoto show in New York. It was in Long Island and we all drove – me, George and Richard were in the car and decided to get off our nuts, so we were in the front row tripping off our tits and shouting things out as models like Ana Drummond walked past. In the car on the way back I was singing 'The Twelve Days of Christmas', but the Boy George version, so 'On the twelfth day of Christmas, Boy George ate in front of me . . . five ring doughnuts, four fried hens, three hamburgers, two Mars bars and a bowl of macaroni cheeeeeessse.' He couldn't bear it – he was just shouting at me to shut up. He got the car to pull over and got out and was crying in a doorway, so I promised him I would shut up if he got back in the car. As soon as he got back in and we started driving I went back at it like the vicious little cunt I was. I drove him absolutely insane.

I think it was the same trip that we went shopping in Bloomingdale's off our faces. There was a little crew of us who had been out partying and then gone back to someone's apartment and everyone had been at the house off their nuts and I was like, 'Come on, I go back to London on Tuesday and I need some Calvin Kleins,' knowing full well that generous George would pay for it. I was earning decent money but if George would pay for things I had no problem with that. I'd always try and nick half his wardrobe too. I just wanted to get out of the house because they were all smacked up and moany, I was the only one high on coke and itching to get out. So I was doing my normal Tony tactic of being a bit like, 'Come out, let's get out of here.' So we were walking down Fifth Avenue in the snow, got to the traffic lights and George was tripping out and started kicking off with a woman on the street – we were a state. I remember being in Bloomingdale's and they shut the section off for us and the woman was like, 'Can I help you?' and George was like, 'Yeah, I'll have a Jack Daniel's and Coke please.' I was just like, 'We're in a shop, George, not a club.' After we left there we went to a tiki bar called Trader Vics with Suzie Streetwalker and Billy Beyond, who were club kids at the time and part of the scene. George bought Suzie an outfit and Billy some Moon Boots. They'd be gauging, which is where people fall half asleep because they're off their heads and you have to kick them awake. A mess.

The last time I went to New York in the 90s, before addiction really kicked in and my world became smaller, was when Trade had gone over to do a club night there and Christian, my boyfriend at the time, had flown out with them. I called him and he was at a house party so, in my paranoid head, I was convinced he was over there cheating. So I got myself on the next flight, stormed into the house and found him in bed asleep. I had caused a massive scene and was obviously completely wrong. We were staying at my friend Vicky Heller's house on Christopher Street so I left and met this hooker with no teeth who invited me to a party around the corner in a place called Boots and Saddles, which was a gay cowboy bar at the time. They were like, 'Do you want to get high with us?' Yes, obviously. So within ten minutes·I was doing their valium, their coke and their ethanol – which you spray on a cloth and sniff. I remember demanding to take over the music and was playing 'MacArthur Park' over and over again. It got to a point when they were like, 'Hey dude, you're going to have to go.' And I was like, 'What the fuck?! You two are kicking me out?' So I nicked their coke and a bottle of tequila and stumbled out on the street. I made it back to Vicky's – just – I think the police helped me back there in the end. Christian and I broke up eventually, but not before I'd tortured him for a few more months . . . Next!

5.

The First Lost Summer

I never travelled well, really. That first trip on Concorde was a bit of a fluke, to be honest. There would always be chaos, there would always be drama, and if there wasn't I would make it.

The first time we went to Ibiza was in 1983. The original crew on that trip was me and Gabby Palomino who ran Models 1. She was a Blitz kid – part of the crew that had gone to the Blitz Club in Covent Garden at the very end of the seventies, who people say started the New Romantic movement – and she was one of my mates from the King's Road. There were a few other people with us but I couldn't tell you who. I do remember that Gabby would go around everywhere wearing fetish gear. We were hanging out with this guy called Brazilio, who Gabby knew and who owned Ku and a few other clubs on the island – he was one of the original big cheeses.

I loved the island from the get-go, it was fucking amazing. We arrived and we were dancing under the stars (Amnesia still didn't have a roof back then), and it was still quite hippy. The clubs were enormous compared to London and they were just huge open-air dance floors. It felt like paradise. Back then you couldn't fly directly to Ibiza, so you would fly to Palma and then change, and people didn't fly as much as they do now, so you really had a build-up. It was so bohemian – imagine going to a beautiful, relatively untouched island in the Mediterranean now, and discovering that they had this amazing party scene with people cut from the same cloth as you? That's what it was like. So luscious and green, with the most stunning deep-orange sunsets. As soon as you landed, it was like a different world, you almost expected Judith Chalmers to appear. The heat would hit you as soon as you stepped off the plane. Ibiza back then was untouched. There were no chains or McDonald's and everything else that there is now. The scene felt very free-spirited back then, and people were really flamboyant. You just didn't have the same vibe in London. I think the first big party we went to was at Privilege, which was then called Ku Club, and I remember I'd been there one night and I disappeared. I ran off with the barman from Ku, which I made a habit of doing in Ibiza – just hopping on the back of their motorbike or moped and disappearing up into the hills for a day or two to do drugs and shag them.

My specialist subject would be getting lost in the hills in Ibiza. I'd either end up at some boy's house or we would be at a party in town and I'd go, 'Come on, let's leave, let's go somewhere else. I know a party happening in the hills.' And then we'd walk out, try to get a cab and walk for miles. And I'd be like, 'It's this way. I know where we are now. I know exactly where we are.' And we'd walk and walk and we'd be going higher. I'd be like, 'Maybe the party isn't this way after all.' We'd be so, so fucking lost. Seriously.

I went back to Ibiza in about '86 with Steve Strange and Rusty Egan and we did a thing called London Calling, which was a club night with a fashion show by BOY London. Rusty and I were there as the DJ's but I never made it to DJ. I met some boy and disappeared off on the back of his moped – again. This time it was for three days. I arrived back at the hotel and got him to drive me around the swimming pool on his moped, with me thinking that I was really fucking fierce. Everyone was there – Paul Rutherford, Jacquie O'Sullivan from Bananarama, we'd taken over that hotel. We were all badly behaved but I think I took the piss, as ever. I'd missed the gig and someone else had to play for me. I was sleeping in the living room of the apartment in the hotel and shagged a boy in Jacquie's bed whilst she was out. I remember her coming back and being like, 'Errmm, why is the lid off my Vaseline?'

The day everyone was leaving, they were all sitting on the coach and ready to go when Steve Strange came up to me and was like, 'C'mon, let's stay here.' I mean, I never needed any encouragement so that was it, we were off the coach and stayed for three months. The owners of Ku had given Steve an apartment to live in but neither of us could drive, so the boy I was shagging, who didn't speak English, became our driver. I was wearing head-to-toe Gaultier when I met him and so was he – that was the depth of our connection. Anyway, he worked at the Coco Loco bar and he just kept giving us free drinks. One of the guys there would make coconut punch and would put MDMA and acid in it and give it out at 1am in the morning and everyone would be off their fucking nuts. One night I remember we were in the car in the hills – I mean these boys drove us everywhere – and Steve Strange picked a fight with one of them and they kicked us out of the car in the middle of nowhere. Steve and I had to walk all the way home. I mean, it was three months of just clubbing and shagging, basically being Tony.

The music scene in Ibiza back then was really quite Euro-trashy. It was the tail end of the disco scene and house music hadn't hit yet. It wasn't the age of the celebrity DJ, that era hadn't started. We had a little repertoire of clubs that we'd go to – Amnesia and Ku, Catwalk in the Old Town and then Loco Mia, which wasn't a club but part shop, part bar and a real scene – and the queens who were the original fan dancers would have crimped, big hair and they'd all wear long black outfits with pointy shoes and huge fans. They were amazing, and the first to do that. Angels was the hot after-hours club that everyone went to. It had these two big podiums which you could stand underneath and look up to. It was all quite debauched, really – I mean it was debauched in that there was so much energy, it was like a world turned upside down, no one was around in the day and then it just came alive at night. The clubs had no roofs, you'd be dancing under the stars and then the sun would come up and you would be with a group of people you'd never met before but who were your new best friends. It was like Gay Utopia, everyone was so, so free, even in comparison to London. For a gay man at the time it was paradise. It was a lot of fun, but it wasn't seedy. Then there were all the little underground clubs, and Pacha, of course.

It was in Ibiza that I had one of the only times in my life I've been violently ill on booze. One night we were at Privilege up on the balcony with some boys who were drinking Chivas Regal. I obviously kept up with them and I remember drinking so much of it that I blacked out and was vomiting. I can remember being in the back of the car with my head out the window, vomiting all the way home along the motorway. We got back to the apartment and I woke up in the morning and I vomited in the swimming pool. And I've never touched Chivas Regal again since. I know this is ridiculous, by the way – I did enough drugs to kill a herd of elephants, but one bad night on whisky and I never touch it again.

I think '89 was the ultimate summer I had in Ibiza. Gina had his birthday party at Amnesia. Alfredo, Danny Rampling and Nicky Holloway were all there. We'd kind of taken over the island. Gina and I had been there for a month already and it was absolute chaos. I'd done my normal trick of disappearing off with a boy and had been gone for three days. I was doing a lot of acid at the time and Gina wasn't, so I'd kind of just found my own people.

So, I'd disappeared with a boy and then gone on to find my friend Nick who was a straight male model. We'd been out for three nights and we'd had a fucking ball – we got each other's humour and had been tearing around the island causing chaos. It was fucking hilarious. We ended up hanging out with this really dodgy group of boys who were using dodgy chequebooks, dodgy cards, everything. I just loved it. I was always drawn to those types of boys, the wrong 'uns. Because they were always the ones that you had the best laugh with.

So me and Nick had come back to the villa and I walked in and Gina was like, 'We're leaving.' And I was like, 'What do you mean we're leaving?' He said, 'We're flying back to

London in an hour, you've been gone for three fucking days.' And I was like, 'Yeah, yeah, fuck off. I'm having a lie down and then I'll pack.' And I remember going into my room, then waking up and it was dark. I got up and I walked around the house and I was like, 'Hello, hello?' And everyone had gone – Nick, Gina and his boyfriend Michael. They had just left me on the bed, covered in my own vomit.

Gina was so fucked off with me. He had left and taken my passport and my plane ticket because I was such a cunt and just left me in the villa. I had no money – nothing. I remember thinking, *Oh my God, what am I going to do?* I did for a moment think, *What the fuck are you doing? You really need to stop misbehaving and sort yourself out.* They'd taken my clothes, they'd taken everything. All I had was one pair of tracksuit bottoms, a Vivienne Westwood pink polka-dot shirt and the Timberland boots I was wearing. The shirt was the campest thing in the world. I was the gayest little cunt, stranded in Ibiza.

I had to wait for Gina to send my passport, which took about three weeks because he wasn't talking to me. I don't know why I didn't just go to the British consulate. In the meantime, I remember walking along the motorway to Amnesia to see Jose and Sandrine who owned it. I went in crying and saying, 'Gina has left me!' And they were like, 'You need to come and stay with us,' and they took me to their house and let me stay with them. I was at their club every night off my nut, but they were so kind to me, letting me stay and giving me drinks all the time. I had no guilt about accepting freebies.

Ibiza really was heaven for someone like me. I had so many Ibiza sidekicks. Andy Stick was a really good one. I'd met Andy clubbing in London. He was this loud-mouthed little shit who just did not give a crap. He would always have sunglasses on and was stick-thin, hence the nickname. He was a good-looking boy and shit did not stick to him. I thought I was bitchy but Andy would open his mouth and it was something else. Me and Andy in Ibiza were pretty ferocious, we'd end up at Bora Bora and be there for three days. I'd be DJ'ing for food and drinks and they'd be like, 'Oh, you going to play for us?' And I'd be like, 'As long as you get everyone drinks and cocaine then I play.' Like a whore. I think the biggest gig that I ever played in Ibiza was probably at Amnesia itself before the roof went on. It was just before the acid house scene kicked off in London and all the acid house DJs were out there. Of course, I'd wangled myself a gig there and I remember playing early soulful house. All the Spanish DJ's hated me because I was playing on their turf.

There were never any drug deaths back then – it wasn't like you heard of people taking pills and dying – because the drugs were so much cleaner. People died as a result of taking them, but not from the drugs themselves. I was forever coming off my motorbike in Ibiza. I'd be tripping off my nut, go down to the roundabout where Pacha was, come off the motorbike and be lying on the road with cars nearly running me over. But I think the first person I remember dying in Ibiza was Steve Walsh, a London DJ, when his jeep overturned.

One of the last times in Ibiza, my friend Cozette arrived. She had worked at the Wag with me doing the door and was amazing – we're still really good friends now. At the time she worked for Jasper Conran and she was the best wing woman. She didn't take drugs and God forbid anyone offer her any – I'd have them – but she could drink anyone under the table. I was very protective of her in a way. Anyway, I'd persuaded Cozette to come out and stay with me, but by the time she got there it was so fucking weird – Danny Rampling's wife Jenni had gone missing and so Danny was refusing to play. With Jenni AWOL, God knows where, and Danny freaking out and everyone around them starting to spin out too, I was like, 'I'm going, babes.' Instead of the week's holiday that she had been promised she got thirty-six hours with me and was then dragged back to London on BA.

When we landed in Heathrow we were going through border control and someone tapped me on the shoulder and they were like, 'Excuse me, Tony?' 'Yeah?' And they went, 'You're under arrest. Come with us.' And I was like, 'Why, what have I done?' I got taken to one side and arrested. I'd been cautioned for possession and had gone to Ibiza rather than report into the police station to sort it out, so I was blacklisted when I landed. I mean, it meant we got a free ride home. I got strip-searched, which wasn't so great, although I pretended I loved it at the time. In the end, I got let off as it was a friend's jacket and I hadn't known it was in there. Funnily enough, the old Royal Courts of Justice where I had to go is now a hotel and restaurant and I went there for the opening recently. I only realised halfway through dinner that the last time I'd been in that building I'd been in a cell and up for possession.

I slept when I got into the police cell. There was never a time that I came back from Ibiza feeling normal and rested, like I'd had a holiday. I always arrived home hungover to fuck and needing a holiday instead. I never ever wanted to leave the island, I would only leave at the very last moment, when I had no money and no choice.

There is one occasion that really sticks in my mind as the worst journey back. As I said, in those days you had to fly by Palma, and then to London. I remember going for my flight back – I'd been out for three days on MDMA and I was off my tits. I was wearing a Jean Paul Gaultier black leather hexagonal black-and-white-football-sleeved jacket, white denim shorts, black Dr Martens boots with the steel toe caps showing and bleached blonde hair.

I got off the plane at Palma airport, went and bought 200 cigarettes and then went to the toilet whilst I waited for my connecting flight – and fell asleep. The next thing I knew I woke up on the toilet. I tried to stand but my legs had gone to sleep and I keeled over on the floor. I tried to open the toilet door and was literally pulling myself along with my hands to get out, when I looked up and saw a guard standing over me.

They were like, 'Hello?' and I was like, 'Huh?' I didn't have a fucking clue what was going on. You know when you've not slept for that long and you spark out, it takes a while to come round. I couldn't remember where the fuck I was at first. They took me to an office where they asked me where I was going. I gave them my passport and ticket. They were talking and looking at each other, then one of them said, 'Your plane left six hours ago.' I'd been on the toilet for six hours, asleep.

I sat in the Iberia office crying until they let me ring my mum. I was like, 'Mum, I'm stuck in Palma. I've got no money. I can't get a flight back until tomorrow night.' There were so few flights back then and I remember sitting there crying, thinking I was in the worst drug comedown I'd ever been in, and my mum went, 'Right, I'm going to ring your Aunty Anne. She lives in Palma, she'll come and get you.' So I was like, 'Okay, thanks,' and stopped crying. Once a mummy's boy, always a mummy's boy.

My Aunt Anne is amazing. She's my mum's sister and used to be a prostitute in the sixties. Although she will say that she was never, ever a prostitute. She was a lady of the night. She had bleached blonde hair and had left London because she was almost notorious as being one of the top brass of the sixties. The papers called her the Golden Girl of Mayfair, and she profited well from it – she had an E-type Jag. If you see old footage of London and Soho in the sixties, there would be sex cinemas and brothels with posters outside, and she was one of the poster girls. So anyway, she left London to move to Spain with all the money that she'd earned from prostitution.

I had to wait for Anne in the airport and there were these little square sofas dotted around. I remember being curled up on one of them asleep and someone kicking me and going, 'Oi! Oi! Wake up you little sod.' And I looked up and it was my Aunty Anne. She had thigh-high PVC leather boots on, and this kaftan top which was all tassels with beads on. She was like, 'Come on, you little sod, what's happened to you? Get up.' I looked up and thought, *Oh my God. I can't fucking believe this.*

We walked through the airport, me in this Gaultier outfit with bleached hair and her with her big bleach blonde hair and outfit, we were a real fucking sight. We got outside and she had this green Jeep with a pink smiling gappy-toothed hippopotamus on it wearing a thong.

My aunt owned some bars in Magaluf with her husband Tino. We drove to one of them where I sat thinking, *Oh my God*. Across the road was the 'Here We Go' bar. And then there was a 'Ben Hur' bar. It was hetero football hell and I was dressed up like the biggest gay you had ever seen in your life. It was like being in Blackpool on a lads' stag do. My Aunty Anne was introducing me to everyone saying, 'This is my nephew, he's in show business.' And she kept making limp-wristed hand gestures behind me, which I could see in the mirror, making out that I was really camp. I mean, I was sat there with bleach blonde hair, a Jean Paul Gaultier leather patchwork jacket, white cut-off denim shorts and Dr Martens steel-capped boots. I don't know what she meant – how dare she call me camp?

I left the bar and went and sat on a wall, praying to God and apologising for all the evil things I'd done in my life, all the times I'd been horrible to people. 'Please God,' I was praying. 'I'll never be like that again. Please get me out of here.' I mean, I was getting homophobically abused, I was on my own, being shouted at: 'You gay cunt, look at the state of you.' I just sat there and cried. Remember, I was on a three-day comedown as well.

Later we went back to my aunt's. She had four dogs and what seemed like about seventy cats. There were animals everywhere. I was like, 'Oh my God, how many animals do you have?' And she was like, 'I got six cats, four dogs, eight ducks and chickens and something else on the roof that he doesn't know about.'

'Doesn't he hear them quack?' I asked.

'Oh no, he doesn't speak any English.' She said.

It was such a mental night, she was mental. The next day she took me back to the airport and she said, 'Tell your mother I hate her.' And as I got out of the car I just thought, *You know what? I fucking love you.*

My Aunty Anne is still alive, she came to see me in London two Christmases ago and I took her shopping to Selfridges and to Harrods with my boyfriend at the time, David. She said to him, 'Has he asked you to marry him yet? He does that to all of them.' When I split up with Johnny, she went, 'Well, you really fucked that one up didn't you? You always fuck it up, don't you?' She's brilliant.

You know, Ibiza is a beautiful place, but all those times I went in the 80s and 90s I wasn't really there. I was living my best life and really helping to put Ibiza on the map, helping Ibiza to become what it was, but I was doing so many drugs and it saddens me, because I just don't really remember it.

When I go back now, sober, the island seems magical. If you take away the big tower blocks and leave the super-clubs you can find parts of the island that still have that beautiful relatively unspoilt Ibiza feel to them. It's stunning.

Just as my Ibiza looks didn't travel very well to Magaluf – I was like an angel fish put in with a load of old carp – another example of my outfits not really travelling well is when I wore head-to-toe Galliano to go to Jamaica. I'd met John when he'd graduated from St Martins with his Les Incroyables show in '84. He used to dress me head-to-toe in certain looks. He gave me a load of sailor tops that were cut and twisted and ruched. He made a stars and stripes outfit for Levi's with Madonna's face on and gave me the one from the ad. People were quite jealous of our friendship at the time because he would give me clothes and I would trot around town wearing them all the time – these mental sailors' outfits – and that's what I was wearing to go to Jamaica with my friend Yumiko.

Yumiko was one of those girls I would have crazily intense friendships with all throughout the 80s and early 90s – ridiculously intense but that would never last that long. These girls would come into my life and we'd do loads of drugs and have these mental relationships then they'd burn out really quickly out or they'd be so intense that the girls would get into a lot of trouble and be stopped from seeing me.

I could be so foul to my female friends. I was a bully and I ruled by being top dog. With Vicky Heller I'd be like, 'You need to do more drugs, you're boring.' I never let Cozette touch drugs ever – and went absolutely mental if anyone tried to give them to her. And God forbid any of them get a boyfriend without my approval, they would be in for it. 'Where did you meet him? He's rent. I've seen him. He's gay, I know loads of guys he's shagged or who've fucked him.' I was merciless until they broke up with them. Byeeee.

Anyway, Yumiko was this rich Japanese girl who was a bit of a super fan and who used to come and see me in clubs and hang around the DJ booth. We did untold amounts of cocaine together. She said she was going to Jamaica and asked if I wanted to go, so I tagged along. We got there and I was wearing John Galliano baby-blue flared trousers and a sailor top with bleach blonde cropped hair and I looked so, so gay. We got to Doctor's Beach in downtown Montego Bay, one of the most homophobic places in the world, and people were calling me names on the street and I'm mincing along dressed as a fucking sailor. We were so much trouble, me and Yumiko, staying in this amazing hotel and doing coke on the beach. Yumiko was amazing, she used to buy me presents from Chanel every week – little bits of jewellery.

There we were, waltzing around Jamaica, spending her money like it was going out of fashion. We met this guy and went to his house in the hills to freebase coke with him. I'd imagined we were going to some luxury mansion, but when we got there we saw a flint cliff with little huts perched on top, and when we got to the top there was his little shack made of wood, like two Portaloos stuck together. We were freebasing coke off an old Coke can and I got so, so out of it that I was like, 'Oooh, I really need the toilet. Like now!' The guy points to a hole outside, so I go and shit in this hole and then I hear all of these noises in the bushes and this massive raccoon shoots out, bites me on the leg as I'm sat on the hole. We ended up going back down the mountain in pitch black and hitched a lift from a lorry to take us to the hospital. I had to have stitches and a tetanus shot. I've still got the scars to this day. Anyway, like anything to do with me, it all went wrong.

We had spent all of Yumiko's money and were stuck there in this amazing hotel in Montego Bay with no money, waiting for money from Japan to hit her account. After about three weeks I'd had enough and came back and I never saw Yumiko again.

That must have been about 1989, just before Gina's thirtieth and the Summer of Love and acid house. I was twenty-five and having the fucking time of my life.

THINGS I LEARNED FROM THE 80s

Remember that you're not the party.

Breathe. For over ten years I never stopped and it was constant. Life isn't a race, you can actually stop and take breathers and nothing's going to change.

Don't mix your drugs like you do your friends. I would take anything with anyone and end up anywhere – it's never a good look. Though I still thought I was fabulous.

Look after your fucking clothes. I had so many one-off pieces that Keith Haring had made for me and I lost them all over London. He painted me a jacket and customised my trainers. I still managed to lose all of them. I remember I went home with one trainer one night, I've no idea where the other one ended up.

Never take Ecstasy before DJ'ing in a field to 50,000 other people.

Never get so out of it in Ibiza that you forget where you're staying . . .

Don't steal your mate's purse then ask them for a tenner to get home.

Don't burn all your bridges because you'll never fucking get back. We're so busy chasing fame and slagging people off that when we need to get back to ourselves there's no way to get there.

6.
Rave On

Acid house was the biggest youth revolution in twenty years – we hadn't seen anything like that since the 60s. Everyone had gone to Ibiza (three years after me, I might add) and having danced under the stars off their nuts at Amnesia to the early house that was coming across from Chicago they came back feeling like they'd been let into the biggest cosmic secret ever, and wanted to share it. *The Times* had just reported the first Ecstasy seizures in London and drug culture was changing. People were switching from doing coke to Ecstasy and MDMA and when you change the drugs, the whole vibe of the scene changes too. So all the guys got back from Ibiza and started to do nights; Danny Rampling started Shoom with his wife Jenni and Ian St. John started Spectrum and Future, which were both at Heaven, and which Paul Oakenfold played at.

Shoom was the first one I heard about. I was still doing all the musical direction for Limelight and the Wag and then people started to say to me, 'You need to come to this club called Shoom, it's totally your thing.' It was over in a fitness centre on Suffolk Street near Southwark Bridge and that was really the start of the whole acid house scene. This was in autumn. The whole Balearic vibe was totally new to London, and when Danny and Jenni started to do Shoom it was really going off. In the end, they had to move venues three times to fit everyone in. So, of course, I went to check it out. House music has always been my first love – we'd started Jungle on a Monday night, which was at Busby's on Charing Cross Road, where G.A.Y. was, and that was the first house night in London. Steve Swindells and Kevin Millins did it, and I was a DJ with Colin Faver. And so, just like before, like the cuckoo I am, I started playing at them all. Suddenly, Danny's name got massive and – lo and behold – we became close again.

At the time I'd been living with a boyfriend called Tom. He was a big love and he played an important part in my life. Over the course of writing this book, I've debated and then debated some more about how much I want to talk about previous relationships, and I think probably not a lot. Of course, I want to recognise each of the loves of my life for the joy and immense happiness they brought, but it's not fair to say anything more. Me? I'll tell you everything, and then some, but I think some things I have to respect. Anyway, I had moved out of Tom's into a flat on the corner of Old Compton Street and Frith Street. The week after I moved in, Jenni and Danny's crash pad got burgled so I said, 'Why don't you come and stay with me?' So they moved into my living room. Jenni was my agent at the time, and we all became the best of friends. You know, at that point in London, I was a big cheese. I was being booked for everywhere and was getting loads of press attention – I remember doing 'A Life in the Day' column for the *Sunday*

Times Magazine. I was lying on the sofa and my mum was sitting on the arm for the picture and I remember saying things like, 'My day starts with a can of Coke and three Nurofen and then I go to my club . . .' I'd go on about how 'I have a room in my friend's house in Chiswick but I don't pay rent, I pay them in my being.' I was such a twat. I was at Tom's house watching TV one night and there was Harry Enfield doing a sketch taking the piss out of me on his programme. Pretending to be a DJ with a Nurofen and a can of Coke . . . I thought, *I've fucking made it!*

Now, in late 80s, the scene had changed massively – it wasn't about being straight or gay. I'd DJ'd at straight clubs, the straight DJ's played at gay clubs. I mean, there were still loads of gay clubs that we'd go to midweek, clubs like Pyramid. The MDMA that was coming in from the States was so clean and pure that everyone was completely loved up. For a moment it didn't matter which tribe you belonged to, you could be a crusty hippy, a football lad, straight, gay, it really didn't matter. I remember being at the Wag Club off my nut on Ecstasy and making up with all these boys I'd hated for years. I met some of my very best friends for that year on Ecstasy. I never saw them after that but they were my absolute best friends for that entire year.

The way we all dressed changed too. Designers had taken a back seat for a little while and it was all about streetwear. It was all about bright colours and loose clothes that you could really dance in, not the trussed-up outfits that we'd all been wearing in the early 80s. I was wearing high tops and tracksuit bottoms. It couldn't be any old streetwear, though, what we wore would be the equivalent of getting your hands on a Supreme drop now – I'd get loads of clothes in New York with the Beastie Boys acting like my personal shoppers.

The smiley face that became so symbolic of the rave scene came about when Shoom changed their flyer to a smiley face early in '88, but everyone was doing them because that's what you did when you were off your nut on E – you smiled from ear to ear.

There were so many scenes at that time, and acid house was at the complete opposite end of the spectrum to fashion and disco. There were underground warehouse parties, parties in basements, derelict buildings, and it built and built until the summer. Suddenly all the bods and DJ's on the London club scene got involved and started throwing parties and car park raves and they grew and grew and grew. I'm sure if you look at a book of flyers from the time it's all the same names playing at a thousand parties. Me, Danny Rampling, Terry Farley, Andy Weatherall, John Digweed, Sasha, everyone was on that scene. George started DJ'ing when he would come to gigs with me and sit behind the DJ booth and sing over the top of records, and that's how his Generation of Love record came about, which became a real rave anthem.

Terry Farley and Simon Eccles had started a fanzine called *Boy's Own*, which was really a kick against Thatcherism. It became a club night and they started organising raves and parties. They would hold parties in fields and take over farms. I remember one where there were about 300 of us, Gina was singing and the police turned up and politely asked what time we would be finished. The parties started getting bigger and bigger and bigger until there were raves up and down the motorway for thousands and thousands of people. In a way the acid house scene was really the start of festival culture as we now know it in the UK.

I was DJ'ing at every rave on the motorway to every fucker under the sun. I DJ'd at Sunrise in Maidenhead to 55,000 people, which was the biggest rave of them all, and it became insane. I remember I was DJ'ing in a field and looking out to thousands and thousands of people. I'd done so much MDMA that I looked down at the records and saw only these huge chrysanthemum heads spinning around. I had no idea what to do with them, I just kept staring and watching them go round. That wasn't an isolated occasion – some twists and turns are different to others. I'd be tripping my tits off and trying to remember the address of a party. I remember being on the way back from a rave with Gina and six other people in an illegal minicab, going back and forth over every bridge in London trying to find the after-party. I'd be going: 'It's near this bridge, no, it's near that bridge,' and we were in the car for two and a half hours and I started kicking off and shouting at the driver. In the end we all got kicked out and had to walk. We never did find the party.

I was dating a guy called Patrick at the time who would drive us up and down the motorway to the various raves. I'd met Patrick through his best mates Mark and Suzanne who worked for Wayne Shyres, a big club promoter. Patrick was straight and I remember the first time I met him I thought he was the most beautiful man in the room, very classically handsome, tall with dark curly hair, beautiful hazel eyes and broad shoulders. We became really close and one night ended up getting it on . . .

My gang at the time was Paul Rutherford, Boy George

and Sam McKnight – people who are still in my life today – with Patrick driving us. We were crazier than a cartload of monkeys. We used to do these weekends away called Chaos down in Pontins and I would do a TV channel in the middle of the night from a makeshift studio on the site. When the party ended you could go back to your chalet and switch on the TV and watch me with all my mates off our nuts. It would just be us being manic in the studio – I'd be getting boys to do the helicopter with their dicks whilst they danced. It was absolute fucking chaos.

We wrote off Patrick's car, his mum's car and his dad's car within about four months. We drove through two bollards and hit a lamp post with the last one. I was such a mental drama queen, I told everyone that he'd tried to kill me and that he was drunk driving, when really it was me screaming at him in the car that caused it. We split up because, like everyone else before, I'd pushed him too far and he'd just had enough. It's like going to the same circus every day for six months – exactly the same act every time, and it's just not funny anymore.

The rave scene only began to become pretty dark when the press started printing that the youth were out of control, and when people started holding massive fucking raves where you had to go to a phone box on the M25 to get directions. That's kind of why it started and ended so quickly. You would turn up at these old aircraft hangers and the quality of people would be terrible. If they hadn't been on Ecstasy, there would have been a mass brawl. By that stage, raves weren't nice or safe places to be.

Those big raves got taken over by gangsters very quickly, and they all got nasty. The Summer of Love came and went and turned into an Autumn of Greed. As soon as people realised they could really cash in, that quickly destroyed everything. The Ecstasy wore off and other types of people were coming out. The villains, the football thugs. The love and the camaraderie of those drugs stopped. People started to do cocaine again and the whole vibe changed. If you go to a party where everyone is on Ecstasy, the vibe is very different from a party where everyone is on cocaine. It's a completely different dynamic with Ecstasy – the effect is always the same, but with cocaine you have no idea what's going to happen – it's a really unstable drug. Alcohol and cocaine – worst combination ever. The acid house scene started to be shut down by the police, and like anything, it became mainstream. You'd see grannies walking down the street in acid house T-shirts and you knew it was over.

The E that had been coming out of the States was so clean and pure, it was fucking amazing. Then it started to be produced here and it just wasn't the same. It wasn't the same buzz – it gave people a nervous, jittery edge, it made people vomit, it felt like it had been cut with speed – and so the scene started to change. As the drugs got cheaper, so did the people – you'd find yourself in the middle of a field with a load of thugs wanting to beat each other up and it got to a stage where you would think, *I don't want to be around these people. I don't want to be here.* That all happened within a year. After that, clubs got smaller and then people wanted to go to places where they could dress up again.

Raves of 50,000 people can't be sustained – it's just human nature. We build these things up, make them big and beautiful, and then they die. That scene might have lasted just a year and it might have started as just a few clubs, but it was an absolute phenomenon. There was a really beautiful moment early on when it was all very pure and very fun, but that was before it was seen through the eyes of the media. Illegal raves were being busted by the police and all of a sudden they were on the front pages of all the papers. Suddenly it became punk rock, anarchy – suddenly it became everything people were scared of. At its heart it was just kids having a fucking great time, and that scares the life out of people. That fear was all media-led, like it is now, but the combination of media fear and the gangsters and thugs moving in to monetise it meant that it only lasted for a very brief moment. Before it got hijacked, acid house was a rebellion against Thatcherism – we had gone through the Poll Tax wars and all of those moments under her leadership and the youth fought back for a right to party and we won that fight. Fucking hell did we.

Acid house never really ended entirely, it just got diluted and grew into other wonderful things. It was the gateway to the opening of loads and loads of house clubs, it brought house music to the masses and it was a job well done. Acid house wasn't about smiley faces and popping E's, it was about the music, some incredible artists, some incredible DJ's and some incredible producers, and it's evolved and lived on in those people – a sign of really good music. Without acid house, we would never have got garage music, and so many other genres that evolved from that moment.

Gina's thirtieth birthday really summed up the rave scene for me. He asked me to host the party for him, so I went to town. We got Judy Blame to design the T-shirt, which was one of the first smiley-face T-shirts. It had a fluorescent pink face with all of these little sperm coming off it which spelled the words 'Fat Tony invites you to Boy George's 30th birthday party' around the edge. We found this dirty old warehouse in Southwark Street, near London Bridge. It was the hottest party you've ever been to, everyone in there was absolutely soaking wet. It was a full-on Ecstasy rave. Danny Rampling, Jeremy Healy and I all DJ'd. In side rooms people were lying on the floor on mattresses. It was the other end of the spectrum to the polished, high-end glamour of the Boy George persona. This was pure hedonism.

We invited 1,000 people and it went on all night until midday the next day. It was such a sweatbox that at one stage I was just wearing three T-shirts – I had one T-shirt on top and then another two that I was wearing as a skirt. People didn't take their tops off during this period. People wore clothes because they wanted to be seen in them. We weren't wearing designers anymore, it was all very relaxed and comfortable, but people would have taken a lot of time deciding what they were going to wear. It was about what you wore and how you wore it. You still had to have the look.

The acid house scene really gave birth to the superstar DJ, and it gave birth to the super-club. For me, those became the motorway years – '92, '93 and '94. We'd be up and down the motorway DJ'ing at different venues and it was a continual party.

I was still living in Soho, above Bar Italia. Jenni Rampling was my agent with Fran Cutler and they would book me and Danny so we could go together. It was what every big DJ at the time was doing, really – the era of the super-club outside of London: Cream and Renaissance and Miss

Moneypenny's. And all of the big London DJ's were being booked to tour and play at them. You'd stop at the service station and bump into other DJ's and be like 'Ohhhh, hi!' And then we'd get back into the car and slag them off, 'Oh, that cunt, didn't he look terrible?' So vile.

We'd be paid a small fortune to go somewhere like Cardiff, though often I'd get there and immediately be like, 'Get me back in the fucking car, get me back to fucking London. I need some fucking drugs. Get me back.' I really was a handful. I'd either have brought drugs with me or would have taken what I thought was a reasonable amount to get me through the night, but we'd get there and I would have done them all in the car. So, I'd ask for more drugs and if they couldn't get me any I would get really angry, refuse to play and storm back to the car insisting I was taken back to London, clucking all the way.

I would argue with everyone, I could argue with my own reflection, I was literally the worst person at that time. I remember once picking a fight with Graham, our driver, who sadly passed away recently. Poor Graham was our long-suffering driver who had been booked by our management companies. He took us up to do a gig at a club in Cardiff, which I'm sure we must have been paid a small fortune for. They had this hideous green room which was like something out of *Brookside*. It had one of those awful seventies home bars – before they were cool – like the one Pat Butcher had in *EastEnders*, with fucking flock wallpaper. I remember the guy who owned it thought it was classy but we were vile and just took the piss out of it . . .

The reason it made such an impression on me was that the guy who owned it was giving us some coke by chopping us a line out at a time. He wouldn't let me buy any from him, or just give me the bag. I mean, giving me a line at this time was a bit like a drop in the ocean – it didn't touch the sides. So I kept asking him if I could buy it from him. I was even saying 'please' and being as nice as fucking pie, which was a rarity at that time. He kept chopping out lines, but obviously that wasn't enough for me, and by the end of it I was fuming. I remember just saying, 'Look mate, seriously, don't be chopping my lines out for me, either give me the fucking bag or fuck off.'

I stormed out of the club, threw the records at Danny, told him to get in the fucking car and for some unknown reason I slammed the boot down without realising that Graham still had his head in the trunk. It split his head open and knocked him out stone cold. He was lying there on the floor covered in blood and I was like 'Oh my God, I'm so sorry,' while at the same time going to Danny, 'How the fuck are we going to get back to London now? You're going to have to sober up and drive.' Danny was saying he was too off his nut but I was just like 'Fucking drive!' Then I was on the floor waking poor Graham up, slapping him around the face, 'C'mon mate, c'mon, you need to get up.' Danny wanted to take him to hospital. 'Stop being ridiculous,' I remember saying to Danny. Honestly, I suddenly became paramedic, doctor and nurse all in one. 'Oh, Graham, you're awake – sorry about that, mate. You all right to drive? Follow my finger, c'mon Graham, pay attention. Okay, he's fine to drive. Get in the car.'

And I made him get back in the car, blood pouring from his head, just because I was so desperate to get more drugs. Once it got a hold of me, there was no stopping it. I had to have what I wanted. I hated going to places where I didn't have my dealer. That's why addicts never travel. If I took drugs with me they'd be gone by the time I got out of the car and I'd be so wired that I wouldn't be able to function. I'd be disconnected from everything, unable to hear the music. It was the worst. Then I'd speed back to London to buy more drugs and get high. That was the cycle. It was a fucking nightmare.

7.

Cara Get Your Coat

The thing is, once you've spent a year dancing in a field, you don't really feel like dancing in a field anymore. You quite like the idea of going back to a club, having a little bit of comfort, a little bit of decadence. It's the way things are, it's a cycle. It always has been and always will be. I feel like I'm on my fiftieth cycle about now.

London was really happening at the beginning of the 90s. Acid house was coming to a close and with it, a load of smaller club nights had emerged, another part of the natural cycle. There were so many little nights that we would all go to – every night of the week there was somewhere else to go. In terms of variety, it never got better than that.

There was Love at the Wag, and clubs like City of Angels, RAW and Pure Sexy. There was a bar called Cruise next to Peter Stringfellow's with pinball tables and we would sit underneath them absolutely off our nuts on E. Everyone else would be cruising downstairs. It was the coolest place to go to. It was a lot of trouble and a lot of fun. This was pre-social media, when people could go and do what they wanted and meet men. It was probably safer than people turning up at random guys' houses off Grindr not knowing if they're going to be drugged. Phone apps have taken away the element of getting to know someone.

For the most part the 80s and the early 90s were all very sparkly, innocent and fun. We'd go out and have an absolute ball. We would meet Chaka Khan on the dance floor then go round to George Michael's house and sit there while his mum was hoovering around us. People became very famous very quickly, but they were still in your tribe and still just your mates. There was a brief moment during acid house, when everyone was off their nuts on E, that all the tribes melted into one, but when we stopped taking E and started on coke again everyone reverted back to their gangs and became judgmental cunts again.

The big, big night at the time was at Café De Paris. Les Nuits du Mercredi had started at the end of the 80s and built and built. It was started by Nick Fry, who was a London club promoter, and he'd loosely based it around French cabaret. Albert from the Bataclan in Paris used to come over and play and I'd play after him. Albert would play French bistro music and French samba and then I would go on and play early soul and then early house. It became such a moment because it really caught hold of the zeitgeist and it was what people wanted at the time. They wanted to dress up, they wanted a return to a bit of glamour and grandeur. Before this, Café De Paris had been just a disused ballroom on Leicester Square. Les Nuits du Mercredi – or Wednesday nights as I liked to call them – really put it back on the map. And you know, that night kind of launched us and put me and Albert on the map as the DJ's of the moment, too. We'd both been successful within the club world but Café De Paris got so much mainstream media attention – there was a scrum of photographers outside the door every week – that it really did launch us into the public consciousness. For a very long time, it was the hardest club to get into in London.

On the back of that came Kinky Gerlinky – it had started small but really just caught a moment and it grew and grew and grew and then ended up in the Empire Ball Room. It was so dressy, you'd see everyone there. It was the first club around that time that encouraged complete freedom, boys dressed as girls, girls dressed as boys and everything in between. They used to have a huge catwalk through the club which everyone would parade up and down on – it was really back to the dress-up days of the early 80s. They were really good times in the respect that everyone cared about what they looked like and didn't really care about anything else. People were over drugs and were back into fashion.

Well, everyone apart from me. I had a dealer called Danny at the time. Poor Danny was long-suffering, and I only remember this because he's now a black cab driver and picked me up recently – completely out of the blue. He said he knew me from back in the day and told me the story . . . I had someone who'd get me coke in Soho and I badgered them to introduce me to their guy. At first they'd said no but I kept on at them until they gave in. That guy was Danny. He wasn't a full-time dealer but did it on the side whilst he worked as a gaffer at the Dominion Theatre. Once I knew where he worked, there was no stopping me. I'd turn up at the stage door halfway through a performance and pester the guys to go and get him. They'd tell me he was working and I'd tell them he wouldn't mind and was expecting me and that it was an emergency. 'You had absolutely no filter,' he told me when he picked me up in his cab.

So there we'd be at Café de Paris, and it was like a *Who's Who* of the coolest people on the scene at that time. On one side you'd have Cameron (Alborzian) who was in Madonna's 'Express Yourself' video with another male model called Moose who was doing every catwalk going at the time, and then on the other side there would be Bryan Ferry and Mick Jagger. You know, we were young and we were fun. We had money and we dressed well and we were having a fucking amazing time. Nellee Hooper was in our gang and was doing loads with Madonna at the time, who obviously we all were really into. It was pure unadulterated glamour and we lived for it.

I had this record called 'Work this Pussy' by Sweet Pussy Pauline. I mean, if you think Cardi B's 'WAP' is explicit, you should listen to this. The lyrics were so foul – it was fucking outrageous. Anyway, I loved this track and one time I was playing it and persuaded Leigh to take his underwear off and as the track got more explicit he started twirling and twirling and his dress was lifting up and everything was going everrrrrrywhere. We were halfway through the track and it had obviously got back to the doorman what was going on. He came running through and didn't know what to stop first – me playing this fucking foul track or Leigh twirling his bollocks, dick and arse around the room. It was fucking hysterical.

Stevie Wonder was in Café de Paris one night and sent one of his guys over to ask me what the track was. I told him and he came over again and said, 'Stevie wants you to give him this record.' I told him to fuck off, and the guy pointed back over to Stevie and was like, 'He's just there, and he wants this record.' I just replied, 'Yeah, I know. I can see him.' That's how much of a cunt I was. Another time I was playing and had been given a preview copy of 'The Power' by Snap! and started it playing and went to the loo, leaving Cozette in charge. I don't think I was gone for that long but she said she had to play it four times . . . I mean, maybe I'd been chatting in the loos, doing a line or getting a blow job. Could have been all three. That was standard behaviour at the time and no one fucking noticed we'd played it over and over again anyway.

Café de Paris was one of those clubs that just grew organically. People assume these places were the centre of everything from the get-go, but they weren't. There would be just thirty or forty people some weeks. I would be DJ'ing at the beginning and Vivienne Westwood would be there with Sara Stockbridge and her crew but that was it – it was literally me, Leigh, Albert and them in the club. The thing about Café De Paris was that it had the right people going from the very start. You have to remember that London didn't have any social media back then but word got around very quickly when something was good. We didn't allow photographers in so no one in there was going to get papped, and it just grew and grew and grew.

Taboo nightclub was yet another club that grew organically. It was only really successful for about three or four months, the rest of the time it was just me, Julia, Jeffrey, David Holah, Leigh Bowery, of course, and the BodyMap crew. But it caught people's imagination for a short while and has ever since. At the time it was seen as so debauched. The first flyers that Leigh ever did for Taboo were white pieces of card with cut-out porn pictures stuck on them. It got into the papers as this place where all the freaks hung out and then that was it, everyone wanted to be there. It got really big and then died just as quickly. Mark Vaultier, who was the doorman there and was well known for confiscating people's drugs and then doing them himself, as well as for having a razor-sharp tongue – 'Would you let yourself in?' – died of an overdose in 1986. Lots of other people started dying and Maximus, the club where it was held, changed hands and that was the end of Taboo . . .

I loved Leigh – we had stayed friends all the way from the beginning – Diana Dogg, the Pink Panther, the Wag, Limelight, right until the end when he died in 1994. He used to absolutely terrorise me, trying to get me to sleep with him. He used to do this whole big 'Come on Tony . . .' thing every time. Leigh out of drag was the scariest thing you've ever seen. He wore a man wig and had holes in his mouth and face where he'd put safety pins through his cheeks. You know, Leigh was just so, so funny. He was a showman at the end of the day. I remember he used to make up names for the guest list to spice it up and add a bit of buzz to the night – a mix of outrageously big Hollywood names and slightly trashy British soap actors. Sophia Loren would be on there, Elizabeth Taylor, Barbara Windsor, but then you almost believed it because people like Britt Ekland actually did turn up. Then he'd spread the word around that they were definitely coming. Club kids still do it today, and it works!

One of my funniest moments with him was finding a bag

of pills in the street after a night out. Someone had either dropped them on purpose or lost them in Leicester Square. Either way, Leigh and I sat on the pavement and downed them. We had no idea what they were – though I was determined they were Ecstasy. Leigh was dressed as a toilet – all in white with a toilet seat on his head, and massive platform boots. It was a major outfit. We'd been at Kinky Gerlinky at the Empire Ballroom, so it was a Thursday morning, probably around 3am. We got totally off our nuts and then went to Pink Panther. I remember us leaving there and getting on the tube with people on their way to work. Leigh was being so, so outrageous and I was pretty outrageous myself. We were staggering, off our tiny little trees, through Berwick Street Market in Soho. Christ, we must have looked a state. We just didn't give a shit.

After Taboo, Cambodia became Leigh's night. It was also his last night before he passed away. Our friend Trojan, Leigh's right-hand man, had already gone. I remember the day Leigh died. It was New Year's Eve, I was at home in my flat on Frith Street when I got the phone call from Sue Tilley, to tell me he was dead. He'd been in hospital for two weeks with AIDS-related illnesses, but it was at that time when those phone calls came a lot. People would keep their diagnoses to themselves, as Leigh did, because they didn't want to be judged. The stigma was still terrible in our own community, let alone outside it. We were all close to him because we all came from that era, but you know, we'd see each other twice or three times a week out and about, but also I was doing my own thing and riding the cocaine rocket at that point. I was fucking Rocketman, I was everything Elton John sang about, all in one dodgy suit. I was living my best life with no electricity in Soho. My priorities had shifted – it was all about partying. That was just what I was, and there wasn't much room for anything or anyone else. Leigh and close friends being ill and in hospital was just background noise. It was common for people to go in and then come back out at the time, you never really knew when it was the end.

All of a sudden, members' clubs were opening up. It had all started with Zanzibar in Covent Garden. Everyone went there and it was the first that did late-night cocktails, which now seems ridiculous, but at the time it was revolutionary. The Groucho followed, opening in '84, and Fred's opened in '89. Dick Bradsell, the creator of the Espresso Martini, was the head barman there.

Rose Freud, who set up Fred's with Fred Taylor, came to see me when they were opening and asked me if I wanted to be the resident DJ. I agreed and though I only played on a Friday and Saturday, I'd be in there all the time. It was the place to be. Me and Neneh Cherry used to hang out there with Ray Petri and the Buffalo Boys – you have to remember that they were the coolest guys on the block. They were on the cover of *The Face* all the time.

Fred's was really wild. It was a tiny club spread over three floors but, to be honest, they were all like corridors apart from the basement. It was on Carlisle Street in Soho and you could just do whatever you wanted. People went there seven days a week at that point. It wasn't about coke or pills, it was about having fun. It was there that I first met Kate Moss, after she had walked in John Galliano's second show. She was just so, so Croydon. She was like 'Alllllrrrriiiiihhggt?' I loved her from the moment I met her.

I used to make her Long Island iced teas and she'd get so pissed I'd tuck her under the desk downstairs to have a sleep and go down every now and again to give her a little kick to check she was all right. You know, Fred's really was the hub of everything at the time, all the creatives that you see out and about now would all have gone there. It was bigger than the Groucho or Soho House in terms of celebrity. It was so small and so exclusive – you had to be chosen for membership – that everyone just wanted to go there to be seen.

People would go to Fred's and then on to the Groucho, and it would be all the usual reprobates. The Groucho was always the first and last stop of my night. Because I lived above it, I don't think I ever went in through the main entrance. If you go into the Groucho smoking area and look up behind it, there's a little wooden bridge and it was across from there that I lived. I'd climb out of my window, across the roof of Ronnie Scott's, over the little bridge and in through their kitchen upstairs. I'd go downstairs, get what I wanted and go back up. Don't mind me! Paul Rutherford lived on Old Compton Street and it was insane. Literally insane. Another trick was to go down to 24-hour Compton's Cafe, pull boys out through the back door and up to my flat.

I'd been freebasing coke since the early 80s. It hadn't taken hold straightaway, but someone had asked if I wanted to try it, and as I am with all drugs except heroin, I was like, 'Sure!' I'd try anything. But I probably started doing it more at this point and it made everything that little bit harder to keep track of. I would be DJ'ing and turn up three hours late. I'd leave my friend Cozette there having to fend off all the organisers asking if I was coming or not. I'd always blame it on the dealer and say that they'd been late, but God knows where I'd been – I might have been having sex, I might have been getting high somewhere and not realised the time. I might have actually been waiting for the dealer, but it's unlikely.

One time, I disappeared off to the dealer's with one of my best friends at the time and we were gone for four days. Her husband and her manager were all looking for her and when they eventually found her, that was it, she was sent away to rehab for three months. That's what happened when you hung out with me! I pushed it and pushed it and pushed it, and somehow got away with it while others got busted and suffered the consequences.

One victim of this who sticks in my mind the most was a friend I had called Cara. She was an American girl who was modelling in London in the late 90s and we'd become best buddies. I mean, the fact that she liked to party as much as me helped. It was when I had my place on Old Compton Street. We'd been at a club and had gone back to mine and were freebasing cocaine. We were already pretty high and pretty twitchy when the buzzer started going. *Fuck, it's the police!* That was my automatic assumption anytime the buzzer went, if we weren't expecting people. *Fuck! Popo!* Anyway, the buzzer keeps going and going and going, and just doesn't stop. We're getting pretty pranged out at this stage so I'm like, 'Fuck. Hide!'

Cara crawled under the table and I hid around the side of the fridge. I mean, they were the shittiest of hiding places. You could totally see Cara and I had only managed to squeeze half my body behind the fridge. Anyway, the buzzer eventually stops and we're like, 'Oomph. Thank fuck for that!' Then there are these thundering footsteps on the stairs and you know that whoever is making those isn't exactly a little sparrow, and then someone starts hammering on the door, massive thuds like they're about to come through. 'CARA, I KNOW YOU'RE IN THERE. CARA! OPEN THE FUCKING DOOR!' 'Fuck,' she whispers, 'it's my dad!' I mean, I'm like . . . what the fuck? Isn't your dad in America, or wherever the fuck you come from? Because you know when I said we'd become really chummy, I had no fucking idea about this girl, her life or where she was from. I didn't even know her second name. If I had, I might not have been so fucking clueless . . . All I knew was that she could take nearly as many drugs as me and that made her the perfect companion. Anyway, the pounding stops briefly. We let out a sigh of relief and then BOOM, the door flies clean off the hinges, some massive security guy walks in followed by one of the biggest, hardest Hollywood actors on the planet. WTAF? 'Cara, get your coat. We're leaving.' And Cara dutifully gets out from under the table, gets her stuff and leaves, eyes to the floor, walking out with her dad and the security guy. I later found out she'd been taken home and sent away for treatment but at the time I was so fucking pranged out by the whole thing I was paralysed, stuck to the side of that fridge for about eight hours. I swear to God, I did not fucking move.

Christ, that decade was non-stop. At that point in time I was doing loads of big celebrity parties. I must have played for Prince about ten times. The Prince thing, it was so fucking boring, I mean, it was amazing but I was booked to play the after-party for Prince, and I did, but he insisted on playing for the majority of it. Seriously, he'd already done a gig and now he did another two-hour set, this time for just 200 people. We were like, 'Is he doing another fucking guitar solo?' I just wanted to get on and play some records.

I played for Madonna twice. The first time it was the after-party for a gig the record label had organised and the second was for her birthday, I think it might have been her thirtieth. Christopher, her brother, had seen me and he basically said, 'My sister's coming and they want you to do her party.' I was hanging out with him at the time. On the day of the party I had to go to the Groucho for a sound-check and all the roads were closed off – Old Compton street, Dean Street – all filled in with those vans with news dishes on the top. Back then, celebrity parties were big, big things . . . I remember thinking I should probably get myself a bag to see me through the night so off I went to my dealer's house in Queensway. I remember telling him that I had to be back in forty-five minutes. So we start chopping out lines and then he gets the bong out and we start free-basing coke.

My set was starting at 7.30 and I was only leaving my dealer's house at 7, totally wired. The cab dropped me at the end of Dean Street and I remember running back to the driver and being like 'I'm DJ'ing,' but the police wouldn't let me through. I got so bollocked when I finally got there. I was so fucked that I was dribbling, I had proper coke face – I would gurn so badly. An added problem was that George hadn't been invited to the party, so I invited him, and unlike a normal person who might just tell their friend it wasn't going to work, I told them that if they didn't let him in I would turn the music off. And so Madonna's brother

Christopher goes and gets him. By this stage I'm really not handling it very well. Totally spangled and just about managing to play tracks into each other without any moments of silence. Just. And so Madonna comes over and asks me to spice it up and I remember telling her to fuck off. 'Did you just tell me to fuck off?' she said. 'No one ever tells me to fuck off. I like your sass. Keep playing.' And high-fives me! Gina was behind me, absolutely fucking mortified. 'I can't believe you just told Madonna to fuck off and that you're still standing here.' He was absolutely horrified. I just didn't give a fuck.

Playing for Madonna was amazing – I might have been fucked, but I was still playing for fucking Madonna. Playing for Prince was amazing, playing for Wham! The Final at Wembley Stadium was amazing, doing their after-party at the Hippodrome was amazing. They closed all the streets of London off. They just wouldn't do that now. It was at a time when celebrities really were celebrities, they were untouchable, they didn't have their Instagram account open to you. They were superstars.

The really sad thing about these times – playing at parties for Madonna, Michael Jackson, Prince and Elton John, moments when you were playing music and making some of the biggest stars on the planet dance – was that they should have been career-defining gigs and magical moments. And they were. . . but I wasn't really there. I was there in body, but I wasn't there in mind. And I really wish I remembered. Of course, I have memories of them, but not the right memories. My mind wasn't engaged, the only thing I was engaged with was drugs.

I was really good mates with George Michael by this point

and all that competitive stuff from the 80s was way behind us. We'd been vile to George because we couldn't stand that he was in the closet, but also you were either in the Boy George camp or the George Michael camp, you couldn't be in both. It was old-school pop rivalry, like the Stones and the Beatles, Blur and Oasis. You couldn't be in the inner circle and be friends with both. George started hanging out with my friends, people like the photographer Brad Branson, and the singer June Montana, and it all changed. There was angst at the beginning because of Gina but then he started coming to the clubs that I was doing and we'd all have loads of fun together. You have to remember that we were living in a time of Ecstasy, it was all about love and everyone was getting on and partying.

After Café De Paris I had started an Abba tribute night at Bar Industrial in Hanover Square with Dave Dorrell. He was a music manager who had done the song 'Pump Up the Volume' with M.A.R.R.S. It was all 70s music. Me and June Montana from the early Wag days used to do it together and that's how it evolved. At that time, clubs were really, really fun, camp and entertaining. George had just done 'Freedom! '90' and would come down with Linda Evangelista some weeks and play. Every week after that it was absolutely mobbed because people were so desperate to see him.

After that George asked me to play at his thirtieth birthday party at his parents' house in Bushy. He'd bought them this kind of ranch and so we themed the party like an old Western with bales of hay everywhere. I went in drag, obviously – a leopard-print dress with two leopard-print bows – and a clutch bag of MDMA. I had massive yellow Vivienne Westwood platforms and was about eight foot tall.

I was with Neil and Chris from the Pet Shop Boys and they didn't even recognise me.

I was doing so much MDMA and everyone was absolutely off their rocker. There's a really good picture of George lying on the floor and me standing on top of him with my foot (and Westwood platforms) on his back. I remember turning up to the party and I hadn't been wearing any underpants. As I was getting changed into drag I realised I needed a pair otherwise absolutely everything would have been hanging out, so I got the guy that I'd taken down there to give me his. Just as he was taking them off and I was putting them on, both with all our bits out, George Michael's dad walks in and catches sight of this eight-foot drag queen putting this guy's underwear on and it really freaked him out.

I took my George (Boy) up to see George (Michael) in Highgate about two years before he died. We'd drifted apart as he was doing what he was doing and I'd been doing what I'd been doing. I'd been at a friend's house who lived nearby and popped around and put notes through his door saying, 'If you ever need any help then please just call me,' and we'd reconnected again. This was probably about six or seven years into my sobriety. We went over and the two Georges got on really well. We got there and GM gave us a tour of the house, like he always did, but BG had never been there before. Then we sat in the kitchen and chatted about the old times, about music, about new music, about gay cruising – we really covered it all. As we left, Gina said he really feared for him and I said I didn't think it would be long before there were ambulances at the house. GM was worse for wear and having lived that life for nearly thirty years it's not hard to recognise the signs. I remember the exact words we said to each other, and it's just so sad that it was true.

People ask if I wish I'd done more to help George, but I don't think it's about doing more – you can't help someone who doesn't want to be helped. I'd been up to Highgate and spoken to him loads of times to see if he was okay, to see if he wanted any help, or if he wanted to come to a twelve-step programme with me. But addiction isolates – it's just you, the dealer, the people you're doing drugs with and the people who want drugs. Throw a bit of sex into the mix and you're lost from society. In the end, he just stopped answering my calls.

DJ SURVIVAL TIPS

Don't take requests.

Pretend you don't speak English. It saves a
lot of small talk.

Tell people to fuck off.

Make sure you know how to read a dance floor. It's your job
to make people dance regardless of age or gender. If the
music you're playing isn't working, change it. If they're
leaving the dance floor, you're doing a bad job.

Never compile a set at home. Because what's in your head
isn't necessarily on the dance floor.

Love what you do.

Never accept drugs from strangers. Especially
if they're hot.

Never turn the music off and say 'No K, no play,' because
people will remember it for years and years and bring it up
at dinner parties. Even Donatella Versace brought it up when
I last said it at Trade in fucking 1988.
Thirty years ago.

Never get sucked off in the DJ box. It really gets in the way
of mixing records.

Remember you're only ever as good as your last set.
Do your job and go home.

8.

London's Burning

AIDS never officially hit London. It wasn't like COVID, it was never announced. At first, people just got ill from pneumonia or they got the flu and then they died. At the start, no one would admit it was AIDS. There weren't specific symptoms, there wasn't a build-up, it wasn't like cancer. And the symptoms that were there were often passed off as other illnesses. One of the most common visible symptoms was KS (Kaposi's sarcoma), which was a skin cancer that gave people big blotches on their face. People would cover these with this thick make-up, which became the biggest giveaway when you saw people out.

The first case in London was recorded in 1981, but it didn't feel like it really took hold until much later than that – around '85 and '86. Up until that point it had felt like an American thing. You had these big names like Terrence Higgins and Perry Ellis who had died, and then all of a sudden it was here. But this wasn't about people being ill and slowly fading away, they were there one minute and gone the next. Suddenly, everyone around us started whispering. People began staying behind closed doors. People didn't want everyone on the scene knowing that they'd caught it, and in a way we all wanted to live in ignorance, there was such a big stigma attached to it. Sometimes your friends would get skinny and disappear and then the next thing you'd hear was that they were dead.

You would be in a club around that time and people would say, 'Oh, you know so and so has AIDS.' I remember being at Ray Petri's house and him telling me that he had been diagnosed, but I'd already heard it from someone else. It's a terrible thing that we saw it as gossip, but there you are, we were young and looking back I think we were scared and so we gossiped, it's what we knew how to do. Even though there was such a stigma attached to it in mainstream society, we had a little more knowledge in the gay community – it wasn't like you were terrified to be in someone's home or around them.

It was awful because it was such a terrible thing to be happening, but still it was fodder for us all. People liked to think that they were keeping it to themselves, but we lived in such a crazy little bubble that everyone knew everyone else's business. The club scene was so hedonistic, there were so many clubs that were men only and that were essentially sex clubs, and there was no such thing as safe sex back then. Guys wore condoms so they didn't knock a girl up, they didn't wear them with guys. People were having the time of their lives, and all of a sudden this new word – AIDS – came along and it shook everyone to the core. The whole scene went from fan dancing to mourning. At first, you didn't think it would affect you, and then one person you knew would get it and then someone else, and then it steamrolled and you'd suddenly realise this wasn't a passing phase – there was no cure, and it was here to stay.

You have to remember that you couldn't have HIV and live with it for years like you can now. You were diagnosed, it went to full-blown AIDS and then you were dead. There was no drug that was going to cure it or buy you more time. You found out you had it and then you were gone. It was so different to now – people were terrified of getting a positive diagnosis so didn't get tested. You saw the pictures of people wasting away in the media and you knew they were going to die. That was it. There would be no last-minute reprieve, it was game over. And we just turned a blind eye because the last thing you wanted to do was admit that this was what was going to kill us.

What's more, people were being put onto different drugs like AZT, which killed more of my friends than AIDS did. It was the first anti-viral drug, and at the time there was nothing else they'd found that had any effect against the virus, and it had taken seven years for them to find that. It was meant to be the saviour of HIV but it completely annihilated a lot of the people who took it. For some, the side effects of it were awful – massive bloated stomachs and redistribution of fat in the body, and in some it would attack the bone marrow, cause chronic headaches, vomiting and muscle fatigue. Everyone was so desperate that they would take anything just to try and slow it down. It worked for some, but for others, the side effects were just so horrific they stopped taking it, but by the time they did, their bodies were already so weak that the damage had been done.

I remember the first funeral I went to for someone who had died of AIDS. There was only one church in London that would deal with the bodies and that was St Cuthbert's in Earl's Court. Earl's Court was an area that had been completely wiped out by the virus. It was the home of the leather scene and they'd all just been taken out one by one. I remember that the guys that had come into the leather shop in the Great Gear Market to buy their leathers and poppers started to disappear, and then one of the boys who worked on that stand died. There was a bar called the Markham Arms on the King's Road, which is now a bank, and on a Saturday afternoon it became a gay bar for the leather clones. One Saturday afternoon they just stopped going. So many people started disappearing – friends like Yallay and Space from the scene, all of these amazing creative fashion guys, just gone.

The stigma around AIDS got worse and worse until it got to the point where people decided that they had to just own it because something had to be done. People started saying, 'Yeah, I've got it.' Those outside of the gay circle didn't understand and were terrified. I remember the media storm around Princess Diana shaking an AIDS patient's hand without gloves on at the opening of a new wing for sufferers at the Middlesex Hospital in 1987. The pictures went around the world – it was a huge deal that she was touching the hand of someone who had it. It was incredible that she did that, and I think if she hadn't, the stigma would have gone on so much longer. I do feel she played a big part in starting to change things.

AIDS really hit home when Tom Hammond, my boyfriend of the time, came back to the flat one night and told me he'd tested positive. He was American and was one of the funniest guys you could ever meet. We'd been together for three years and as well as being funny as fuck, he was so, so talented. He was an artist who would work on interiors – he would create huge murals on people's walls and floors. He was so handsome, with a massive smile, dark brown hair and big brown eyes. He was the same height as me – six foot one – and always wore diamonds in his right ear. He was another one that I met and fell in love with straight away. I remember being in bed when he got home, and he was absolutely smashed. He'd been at the piano bar where you'd sit around singing with drag queens and he said he had something to tell me – that he was HIV positive and that I needed to get tested. At the time I was completely numbed by it. I'd known we'd been cheating on each other for a long time, so the possibility wasn't a surprise, but it's strange how the mind works. I went into full denial and just shrugged it off. I remember going for one of the first antibody tests about six months later and it came back negative. I was so relieved even though I'd been in such denial around the whole thing. It was harrowing watching Tom deteriorate – he lasted about a year and a half from his diagnosis to death. He just got skinnier and skinnier and weaker, he had skin cancer and had to use a walking stick. I'd distanced myself – he didn't want me there to see him deteriorating and we'd split up, I'd moved into a flat a few doors down. I remember us desperately trying to keep him alive until his parents got there from the US. It was heartbreaking. We used to call each other 'goat' and I remember saying to him, 'Come on, you old goat, you've got to hang in there,' and he replied to me, 'No, you're an old goat,' and that was the last thing we said to each other. He lasted until his parents made it to him and died very shortly after.

I was a mess after that. I organised the funeral in full-on Tony mode – shouting orders and generally being over the top, making sure that there weren't just flowers but lots and lots of flowers – lilies and ivy – on the end of every pew. It got to the point where the vicar called me and told me I couldn't put any more in there. I got Gina to sing and I brought in Carol Leeming, who was the vocalist on 'Joy' by Staxx – one of my favourite tracks at the time – to sing 'Amazing Grace', and I made it an occasion. Now, when I think about it, I don't know if that's what Tom would have wanted, but that's what he fucking got because I was in charge of it. It was never going to be a subtle, quiet affair. It looked like a fucking wedding.

The arrival of AIDS was the turning point in my using, too. It might sound obvious but losing people around me really affected me and I wasn't coping. I very much had a 'Fuck it' attitude to life. I was so reckless and I wanted to live for today. It was about having as much fun as possible – I started to create this persona of the Pied Piper of fun, and I became that person. I'd been that character before, but he became amplified, and he was on all the fucking time. I lost the fucking plot. I'd just be at home playing George Michael on full blast and having eight-balls of coke delivered – which is a fair amount of coke – in the morning and then another delivered that night so you can imagine how much I was doing, mainly on my own.

My own HIV diagnosis didn't come for another decade and when it did, it hit me like a fucking steam train. It was 2001 and my mum had come round to the house I was living in – which I'd basically made into a drug den – and found me unconscious on the floor. My mum knew enough about HIV and enough about my lifestyle to know that she needed to get me to the hospital or I would be gone. By rights, I really shouldn't be here – most of my circle from that time are gone and even if the HIV hadn't got me, then the drugs should have. My mum had seen the news but she also had a gay son. She was so clued up about my lifestyle and my friends and about people dying. My mum probably knew more about AIDS than I did because she'd done her research while I'd put my head in the sand. I didn't want to know. I was in complete denial. I weighed about six stone and had got septic gums from taking too many drugs. In case you don't know, cocaine makes your gums recede and I was taking it every day, so my gums were pretty fucked. I was dehydrated, my mouth was on fire the whole time and I'd get infection after infection because I was sticking my dirty fingers in my mouth. It was sepsis – the poisoning of the blood – which had taken hold, and I was rushed to hospital. They took me to St Stephen's Hospital next to Chelsea and Westminster and did a test, which said I was HIV positive.

I was delirious and refused to believe it, demanding that they discharge me. I was like, 'Fuck off and let me go. I'm not fucking going in.' But I didn't have much choice in the matter. I was too weak to discharge myself and I wasn't going anywhere.

I'd been to the GUM clinic next to Chelsea and Westminster Hospital before – they don't really call them that anymore, but it was the sexual health clinic for genito-urinary medicine. Back then, it was only when you were admitted next door, onto the second floor, that you realised you were in trouble. FUCK. You're sitting in this waiting room with a black wall with clear plastic stars all over it which represent the people who had been there for treatment and who had passed away, and then on the other wall were the stars of people who had donated to the ward, and all of the time you're sat there just going, 'Fuck. Fuck. Fuck. Fuck. Fuck.'

They put me on the Thomas Macaulay Ward, which was the main AIDS ward in London back then. Elton John paid for the kitchens and the food made on the ward – even in those early days, they understood that your recovery, or how well you reacted to treatment, went hand in hand with diet. I was there in isolation for four or five months because my immune system was so far gone. I had full-blown AIDS, and it had already reached my brain and they had to keep giving me lumbar punctures to drain the fluid from it. In most cases that would have been tantamount to a death sentence, but I was lucky that when I was diagnosed they sent me straight up to the research department and put me on a clinical trial for Trizivir. There was this amazing nurse, James Hand, and I remember him saying, 'What's the worst that could happen?' They put me on it and it saved my life.

People had to wear full PPE, not for them, but because my immune system was so fucked that if I caught even the slightest cold it would kill me. I was so fucking humiliated by it. I thought that this was it, I wasn't going to come back from this, this was how I was going to die. Then I got pneumonia and was unconscious for four days. My multi-viral load from AIDS was in the billions, I had under 100 T-cells – the cells that make up your immune system – and the T-cell count of a healthy person is between 500 and 1,200.

They told my mum and dad that I wasn't going to make

it, and I was read my last rites. I'd been to Sunday school as a child but always saw it as nothing more than my mum and dad wanting us off their hands for a few hours at the weekend and the house to themselves, but funnily enough, when you're looking death in the face, you're suddenly more willing to believe in God. My family and close friends all came to the hospital to say goodbye. They'd kept it under wraps what I was in there for – AIDS really wasn't a badge of honour. I remember coming round two days later. My mum was there holding my hand and I was like, 'What's going on?' It felt as if I was lying there for days, with my eyes open but unable to move, but it was only minutes, I'm sure.

Even though I was one chill away from death, as soon as I was conscious enough to talk, eat and feel a little more like myself, all I could think about was drugs. All the time. I remember being stuck in bed and spending all of that time plotting. As soon as I could walk, I was down on the street at midnight waiting for the dealer to arrive. I'd do lines of coke and drink Jack Daniels in the bathroom. Johnny, my boyfriend, came to visit and he said I looked like I had coke on my face. I said not to be ridiculous and that it was face cream. An almighty row ensued. 'Ask the fucking nurses if you don't believe me!' I screamed. Even a hospital ward couldn't make me keep my voice down. He stormed out and didn't come back for three days and when he did he told me not to bullshit him and that he knew that I was doing drugs. I remember one night I had run out of coke and I was out on the street – I had rung the dealer and he said he would get there. There I was with a drip in my arm wearing a hospital gown asking strangers for cigarettes. I remember praying to God to help me to get these drugs because again, I believed in God for that moment. I always believed in God when I was waiting for the fucking dealer to arrive. And then along walked Julie Anderson. She was one of my oldest party friends. I remember her walking down the street and I was like 'Julie, Julie! Thank God!' She took one look at me and said, 'Tony, what the fuck happened to you? 'Oh, don't worry about that,' I said – of course I did – 'Have you got anything?' She was like, 'Tony, you look awful. Babe, you need to go back inside.' 'Don't mind that,' I said again, 'have you got anything?' I thought good old Julie might have some coke in her bag, or at the very least a bottle of vodka. She looked in her bag and I thought, *Thank you God*, and she pulled out a little white Narcotics Anonymous keyring and placed it into my hand. 'What the fuck is that?' I asked. 'It's an NA keyring, you need to go.' Fucking great. 'Oh fuck off, Julie,' was all I could muster as a response.

Fucking Julie. She left me there, and that was the first of those godly moments where someone was there at just the right moment. The dealer didn't deliver any coke that night. I was exhausted and its power over me was spent. Julie had burst my fucking bubble.

9.
Fierce Child

It was whilst I was working at the members' club Fred's in Soho that I got my big music break – although I didn't realise it at the time. There had been all of these bitch tracks which had started to come out of New York, which were dance tracks with drags queens doing the vocals, which were normally foul and funny. One of those queens came over to London and was like, 'That's fierce, child!' and so I and a guy called Rod Lay started a night at Milk Bar called Fierce Child based on the New York bitch track scene. It was down the alleyway between Soho Square and Charing Cross Road, and Ghetto was around the corner – at the time Milk Bar was one of the hottest clubs in town. Danny Rampling, Pete Tong and Paul Oakenfold all had nights there as well. It was 1994 and everyone still went out every night of the week.

I was running Fred's one night and talking to a music manager called Mack who managed a load of 80s bands like Animal Nightlife. He was a big music manager at the time, and I was telling him that I wanted to start recording some tracks and he was like, 'All right then, let me do it with you.' He hooked me up with a producer called Tommy D who was the guy who had done a load of stuff with Nellee Hooper, and Right Said Fred's 'Too Sexy', which isn't really a badge of honour but we won't go there . . . Mack put Tommy and me in the studio together and came up with Fierce Child in about three hours. The concept was simple – Tommy would write the music, I'd write the lyrics and we'd get a queen who could sing to do the vocals. Tommy was so straight – he was the complete opposite of me – but it really worked, he was so much fun.

Tommy and I had a writing day together and wrote 'Men Adore' . . . which ended up being our first track. Tommy and I wrote the music and then I went into the next room and wrote the lyrics in about ten minutes flat. By God, the lyrics were absolutely foul:

'Boys, over here . . . Do you have cash? Cassshhh? Hello? You like what you see, you like what you hear? Men adore, men adore, men adore, a whore. Helloooo Daddy, I'm a whore. I'm a whore. Men adore. Letting men lick my gash, just for the cash. Just for the cash. Hello boys, over here . . . Yes, my measurements are 34-24-34, just the right size. Fierce child, fierce child. Don't fill my ass. Just walk on past. Good sex is what I preach. I'll take you to places you've never reached.'

I mean, seriously. And it didn't stop there, on and on they went:

'Let me feel that cock, twelve inches, is it thick? Is it thick? If you have the cash, you can feel my gash. I'd rather rim a hole than claim the dole. This isn't Russell Square, girl. Cash. Hello Daddy. A whore, a whore. Nine inches or more. I'm a whooooorrreeeee. Fierce child. Yes, it's for sale, £100, £100.

Money well spent. It pays my rent. Men adore a whore.'

When it came to it being played on the radio we had to do a whole new clean version and changed it to 'Men Adore Couture'. There's no way they would play the original.

I'd written the lyrics to the song but we needed someone to lay them down for the track. I knew this American queen called Michael Pattinson, who I'd met back in the day and we all called MP. He was best friends with the artist Jean-Michel Basquiat, and when Basquiat came to London from New York, MP would come with him. You see, the thing with Basquiat was that, even though he was a thing on the scene, we didn't love him – he was actually a bit depressing, but we loved her (MP). I mean, she was the vilest queen to ever walk the earth, but she was fucking fabulous, and we really didn't have any issues with someone being vile back then. I think she's back in New York now.

Anyway, I got MP to come into the studio and he came in and tinkered with the lyrics a bit and then we recorded them. We wrote a B-side together which we called 'Every Queen has his Day' which, to be honest, kind of summed up our lives back then when we weren't in a club. It went:

'Breakfast in the morning, tea at twelve, *Home and Away*, *Emmerdale*,' so far so good, '. . . in my villa all day, waiting for the phone to ring. *Oprah* at five, *Vanessa* at one, lounge, lounge, lounge, book to read, paper, post in the mail, bills, bills, bills, BT, it's £400, I was gossiping with all my New York international girls, BT, she worked me. *EastEnders* at 7.30.'

I mean, it's ironic that we wrote about getting a BT bill in the post – I'd never paid a bill in my life.

So we made the record, and I started playing it at clubs

and we took it out to try and get a record deal. I remember we took it to four record companies – two of them said they loved it but were on the fence in terms of a deal, one of them said they couldn't sign us as it was too rude and the fourth was Big Life Records which was owned by Jazz Summers and Tim Parry. Jazz had been involved in the early days of Wham! and he absolutely fucking loved it. You know, people had heard those New York bitch tracks but no one had heard a British track that was this outrageous about being a massive whore. It really was great fun.

MP and I started doing PA appearances, me behind the decks, MP on a mic, with us both wearing Mark Powell suits and Philip Treacy bowler hats. MP would be in a bright red suit and I'd be in a bright pink one, with Frederick's of Hollywood heels. That was our look – it was major. We did a shoot with Zanna who had made the 'Stars' video for Simply Red, and she shot us for *The Face* and I got my hair dyed tiger, which took about seven hours because they had to do all the different shades one by one.

At the time it was all a really big deal. We had so much press, and the personal appearances for the promo were outrageous. MP would shout the lyrics, 'Let me feel that cock' and then rip out this massive twelve-inch black dildo and people would be really shocked by it. We went everywhere, Heaven, all the big clubs. It was a smash dance hit, and then it was licensed to lots of bitch track albums all over the world. We had a hit on our hands.

The record deal was for three singles and an album, and I can't remember exactly what we got paid but it was a fucking fortune, and this was on top of me already earning good money as a DJ. I managed to buy a house with it, but

I wasn't allowed to have the cash – I remember my manager at the time was all, 'No, no, no. We'll get the house for you, but you're not having the cash.' I was loaded, but I was burning through so much money back then.

My house was on Queen Square in Holborn. You went to the bottom of this beautiful sunken Italian-style garden and there was a Grade II listed cottage, it was amazing. It looked like a country cottage in the middle of central London. That's what I'd managed to buy with the money from the record deal.

A side plot to all this was that I hadn't paid rent in Soho for over three years. I'd moved from place to place and managed to avoid the landlords, but I owed Paul Raymond who owned half of Soho over a hundred grand. Anyway, around the time of Fierce Child, I'd moved out of Soho and I'd bought the house but we were in the papers all the time doing press for the record. The *Guardian* did a full page on me and in it I said that I hung around a lot in Freedom Bar, which was Marc Almond's bar at the time. Anyway, this was the time that I had my tiger-print hair and you could see me a mile away. These two really good-looking guys came into Freedom Bar and shouted over to me. I was like, 'Hiii, how are you?' So the hot guys walked over to me, served me the writ and said, 'We'll see you in court.' They knew exactly what they were doing and I fell for it – all they'd had to do was hire hot bailiffs to catch me out. The next day I got my friend to get his hair dyed the same as mine and say, 'Look, someone handed me these papers last night but I'm not Fat Tony, I've just got the same hair as him.' They were filing for bankruptcy against me. I was fucked.

I remember John James, who was Paul Raymond's

right-hand man, had come to see me loads of times at the flat. He'd be like, 'What are we going to do, Tony? You owe us rent and you've not paid anything. Why haven't you done anything?' I just told them that I'd spent it all on cocaine. I think he was just shocked that I was so honest about it.

We had agreed to sort some payments out but I just ignored it. I'd moved from flat to flat to flat within Soho and dodged them for four years. I'd had to give them the slip so many times, they were calling the clubs I was working at, then they started visiting the clubs. The owners and managers would call and say that someone had been looking for me. There were loads of times when I had to go out of the Groucho and over the roof because they'd come in looking for me, and plenty of times I would hide in the toilets because they'd come in. I've no idea how I got away with it, I kind of think it was because I had the audacity to get away with it. They were really on my case, but rather than freak out because I had fucked off the guys who owned half of Soho, I just thought it was funny.

Aside from the additional income, I was in so many magazines, *The Face*, *NME*, I was doing radio interviews and I had really bought into my own hype. Fierce Child was another turning point in my using, helped by the fact that I had so much disposable income. I was doing an eighth of coke in the morning and an eighth in the evening, so about seven grams a day. Most of the time it was just me on my own, and sometimes I'd run out in the evening and get one for overnight. I always had all the best dealers – I'd become a master of it. When I found a dealer, I'd run them into the ground. An eighth was £150, so when I say I reckon I've wasted a million pounds on drugs in my life, I'm not

'Dusty Springfield' campaign for Joseph Tricot by Michael Roberts '86

On tour with Michael Clark & the BodyMap crew

How to get into clubs according to The Face

Fight with George Michael!

Debi Mazar, George & Madonna at The Groucho Club 1987

Teaching George how it's done...

Ibiza madness with MC Kinky,
Steve McGuire & Louise Prey

With Rosemary Turner at Cafe de Paris

With George at Amnesia Ibiza 1989

With George, Jean-Paul Gaultier,
Gerlinde & Tasty Tim at Kinky Gerlinky '90

Down the disco with Leigh

KARMA PRODUCTIONS
PRESENT
ENERGY

SATURDAY 27th MAY 1989
Bank Holiday Weekend

NICKI HOLLOWAY
STEVE BICKNELL
JUDGE JULES
MRC

PAUL OAKENFIELD
JAZZY M
FABIO
TREVOR FUNG

EVIL EDDIE RICHARDS
FAT TONY
C.M. JARVIS
J.C.

SATURDAY NOVEMBER 5th	YOU ARE INVITED BY	SATURDAY NOVEMBER 5th

SUNRISE III
'THE GUY FAWKES EDITION'
10 pm – 10 am (12 hours)
IN LONDON

MULTI COLOUR LAZERS

ACTION FILMS

Steve Proctor
Eddie Richards
Terry Farley

7 DANCE PLATFORMS

COLLECT YOUR TICKETS FROM:
LONDON JAM CO./68 Berwick Street, Soho, W.1.
BLACK MARKET RECORDS, 25 D'Arblay Street, Soho, W1.
ISIS JEWEELERY, 3 Portobello Green, Under Westway, W.10.
NO INVITE – NO TICKET
TICKETS ARE ONLY AVAILABLE TO GUESTS
OF THE STAFF, MANAGEMENT & D.J.'S OR
SUNRISE CLUB MEMBERS

INFORMATION
01-439 6145
01-734 4801
0296 714949

VARILIGHTS

20K TURBO SOUND

Trevor Fung
Fat Tony
Phil & Ben
Spin-In
Musicians

A LONDON JAM
CO. PRODUCTION

---

and
'SIN'

A 'FLASHBACK'
A night of Acid House,
Balearic Beats and records
that warped a whole generation

PART 1

Boxing Day Dec. 26th
(Bank Hol. next day) 10pm 'til 6am
London Astoria,
157 Charing Cross Rd W1
071 434 9592

DJs:
PAUL OAKENFOLD
NICKY HOLLOWAY
PETE TONG
ALFREDO
JAZZY M
FAT TONY
COLIN HUDD

'Turn on tune in and get right on one matey'

CRAZY CLUB
P A R T
FRIDAY 19th
JAN 1990

ONE OF A KIND

AT
BUSBYS
10pm-3am
157 CHARING X RD WC2
DEX MAIN - DANCEFLOOR

DOWNSTAIRS
SPECIAL GUEST DJ
FROM THE USA +
FAT TONY
ALEX (K.L.F)
UPSTAIRS
alex.p ~orin~
alex (k.l.f)- top buzz

FROM THE PEOPLE
WHO BRING YOU
RAVE ON-SUNDAYS
CRAZY CLUB MEMBERS £
NON MEMBERS £7
FREE MEMBERSHIP
AVAILABLE ON NIGHT

NEW YEARS EVE

YOU ARE INVITED BY
GENESIS
SUNSET
TO
'THE FINAL PARTY'
LEASIDE ROAD, UPPER CLAPTON ROAD.

TOP D.J's
Eddie Richards
COLIN HUDD · PHIL & BEN
Terry Farley   FAT TONY

20K TURBO SOUND

INVITE ONLY
10:00 – 10:00
P.M   A.M.

THE MANAGEMENT RESERVE THE RIGHT TO ADMISSION
STRICTLY OVER 18's • LIABLE TO BE SEARCHED AT DOOR

THE FUTURE IS

ATMOSPHERIC EXPOSURE

PRIVATE PARTY SATURDAY SEPTEMBER 16

SOUNDS AND LIGHT
VOLUME: 30K TURBO
LIGHT: 25K LAZER FX
: DIGITAL DAZZLER
: NEONS
: PROJECTIONS
: ILLUMINATIONS
: BUBBLES
: DRY ICE

ROCKIN ALL NIGHT
DJ COUNTDOWN
10 KID BACHELOR
9 FABIO
8 JUMPIN JACK FROST
7 GROOVE RIDER
6 FUNKY DREAD
5 FAT TONY
9 PIED PIPER
3 PAUL OAKENFIELD
2 PAUL ANDERSON
1 CHRIS ANGEL
+ LIVE P.A's

THE FUTURE IS

UNIT 4

Tuesday 31st January 1989 A.D.

Old Burlington Street, London W1   Tel: 567 6767 for invite & info

DJ'S
TREVOR FUNG
FAT TONY
STEVE PROCTER
FABIO
GROOVE RIDER
L.S.P
LINDEN C
LENNIE DEE & GUESTS

INVITE ONLY - PRIVATE PARTY
ENTRANCE £5.00
9pm START

KU Ibiza

WILD WAVEMACHINE SOUTH SAUNAS

WET WORLD
THE
BERMUDA

TRIANGLE

Come in from the cold to 84° degrees of heat & happiness
Saturday 10th December, The Fulham Pools, Little Road SW6
Doors open from 9pm–1.30am Bring swimsuit,
towel, sense of humour & enthusiasm

... UK FIRST ★ "GIANT SUPERBOWL" WATERFALLRIDE ★ UK FIRST ...

SPACE

SPACE   SAT - SU
4.30am - 12 MIDI
AT BUSBY
157, Charing Cross Road, London W

FAT TONY   ALEX P
STEVE LLOYD   JUSTIN CANTON
NORRIS WINDROSS
Two Floors of Top Music, Top People & Top Atmosp
Get on Top of your Space.
Space Baby's Full Continental Breakfast
available All Day

Down the disco with George

Shouting on the mic...

Trojan's funeral with Lee Sheldrick
and Leigh Bowery 1986

With Mum in The Sunday Times mag

A right pair of geezers!

With Patrick Sheilds

Promo shoot for 'Fierce Child' 1995

The 'other' Pet Shop Boy!

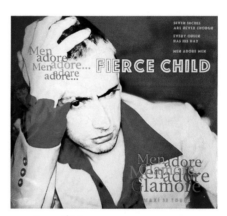

Men Adore....

With M.P & Tommy D

George promoting my record

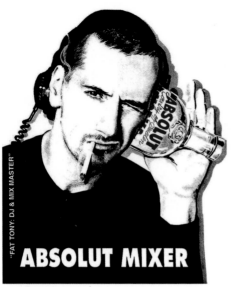

"FAT TONY: DJ & MIX MASTER"

ABSOLUT MIXER

*Absolute Vodka campaign by
Brad Branson & TradeMark*

*Trade's 2nd birthday with
Laurence Malice*

With Paul Lonergan

In full addiction

With Paul Rutherford

exaggerating. I tended to snort predominantly – if you're freebasing you burn through it, quite literally, much more quickly. I would only be high for two hours and the come-down would be horrific.

I would take temazepam and downers when the paranoia got too much and it was about this time I really got into them. I don't remember when or where was the first time I took Rohypnol but I remember the feeling. The drug was all over the press and everyone was going on about date rape drugs, and how you couldn't function on it. I'd just be like, 'What are you going on about? One Rohypnol? I've taken five.' People would take it and it would knock them out. I'd take it and would go out clubbing. I remember feeling the first one and thinking, *Wow . . . this is insanely brilliant.* I couldn't feel my legs and I felt like I was floating. I'd always liked the feeling of a downer. I used to buy friends' prescriptions off them for things like temazepam. I loved being high but I loved a downer to level me out. Rohypnol soon became my downer of choice. I remember sitting with a very well-known friend outside Angel tube station, both off our nuts, waiting for the Rohypnol man to deliver. We were sat there in broad daylight looking like a pair of fucking cunts in fancy dress trying not to be obvious, waiting for our dealer. We couldn't have been more obvious if we'd tried.

That point was really bad. I still hadn't been diagnosed with HIV at that stage but I'd lost Tom and the AIDS epidemic really had a grip on London. I always pretended that it didn't affect me. I had created this persona which was all about having fun and not caring about anything and that was what was expected of me. But I was a fucking mess.

I'd turn up to work after not sleeping for three days and by the time we came to do the second track, I was so far gone that it was an absolute joke. I would do PAs and I wouldn't even be able to speak, I'd just be a slurry mess.

I would play George Michael's 'Fast Love' and Mary J Blige's 'No More Drama' on repeat over and over and over again. I felt like 'Fast Love' had been written for me . . . because it was kind of the story of my life. George told me what he'd written it about, and it was all about cruising and casual sex. That whole album, *Older* and those later albums that he wrote, I really understood them because he had told me what each song was about and it was as if someone had opened the book on me, I really related to it.

The lyrics of 'No More Drama' resonated with where I was in life. I was so, so tired, I was exhausted by the drama of being me. I'd be at home trying to find every way possible to create drama because the more drama going on, the more excuses it gave me to be the mess that I was. I wanted the song to be played at my funeral as my coffin disappeared behind the curtains for the cremation. I mean, seriously, I would sit there and obsess about it. I would play the tracks on repeat and so loudly that my neighbours and the teachers from the school behind would come over and ask me to turn it down, I'd just scream at them, 'Fuuuuuuuuucccck off!'

This was the point when drugs became a really big problem. I stopped paying the mortgage and was evicted. I think I'd paid three of the mortgage payments and they were going to repossess it and I just thought, *I'm not hanging around for this*, and so overnight I fucked off. The only piece of furniture I took was the mirror that I was using to do drugs off. I bagged my clothes and left the TV – everything. I was earning good money so in my head I just thought that I could get it all again.

I seriously didn't understand what bills were. They send me a bit of paper asking for money? Fuck off. I just didn't care. I was so far gone into partying and addiction at that stage. As Gina always said, I was surrounded by yes people and you couldn't get near me to have a word. The people around me would do anything I said.

I never saw losing the house as a problem, I looked at it as, 'Ah well, that door has shut, another one will open.' My friend Wayne Shyres had an empty flat in Brick Lane and so I moved in there for a few months. That was the start of me moving from one friend's to another's, month by month. I didn't quite realise what was happening until the places I was moving to became smaller and shabbier, and the rooms became more and more like cells. Even when you have exhausted every avenue, you make new avenues.

I had started seeing this guy called Christian who I had met at Fred's. He looked like a young George Michael and obviously he was The One – I was in love. I was living in Wayne's place rent-free. I still hadn't learned anything and I still had no concept of bills. I didn't live a normal life. I remember the school near Brick Lane had thrown out their Christmas tree when they'd broken up for the holidays, I found it in the street and took it home and was like, 'Ooooh, I've got a Christmas tree!' I mean, what the fuck? I was spending thousands of pounds on drugs but I had to nick a Christmas tree off the street. At one point, I had a telly that only had half a screen. The only person I spent that Christmas with was Christian. I spent a lot of my time when I wasn't out clubbing around Christian – I didn't really have a lot of friends who I saw outside the clubbing world back then. My life was so full of people all the time that when I wasn't out and was on that comedown, I would just want to be around that one person who could look after me. I didn't want anyone else around. I never saw my family at Christmas at that stage – that was a no-no. I think that year I mainly slept.

I stayed at Wayne's until he sold the place then I moved into the Plaza Hotel or somewhere like that in Clerkenwell because Turnmills and Fabric were just around the corner. Then I'd go from friends' to friends' to friends'. I just didn't give a fuck. I used and abused and moved on. I would travel up and down the motorway, DJ, and the rest of the time I would think about drugs. To avoid the horrific comedowns, I would just buy more drugs and keep going. Uppers and downers on a loop. That was the cycle and it was a nightmare. I was such a cunt to my mates if any of them didn't do what I wanted – I'd throw people out of parties, out of my house, tell them to fuck off and insist no one could talk to them anymore, I'd bar them from Trade and anywhere else I was playing, freezing them out for weeks before I'd let them back in when they had something I wanted – drugs – and then it was someone else's turn to go under the bus.

I'd got to the stage where I'd started to think, *I can't do this anymore*. It would be a Wednesday night and the comedown would be so severe that I would get more drugs to numb it all. Emotionally, I was fucked, in self-destruct mode and completely out of control.

THINGS I LEARNED FROM THE 90s

How to spend vast amounts of money on nothing.

How to lose houses.

In a way the 90s were actually really good for me, you know. I had a record deal, I had gigs everywhere. I learned how to manipulate people to believe in me.

I really learned to connect with music in the 90s. I was completely obsessed with early house until that obsession moved on to drugs.

I learned just how powerful grief can be. Between 1992 and 1996 was when AIDS really hit London and wiped out the gay community.

I learned shame. With the AIDS epidemic there was so much shame projected onto our community but through that I learned the importance of unity within a community because everyone really did pull together.

The 90s was the decade when I learned that it wasn't all about walking into a shop and buying everything and learned that you didn't always have to wear head-to-toe designer, you could just wear jeans and a check shirt and be enough. Sometimes.

I learned how to run for buses in heels. I went everywhere in stilettos, the shoe was a big thing for me in that decade. I'll probably bring them back out again at some point, maybe in my eighties.

I learned how to lose friends and people that I loved.

10.
Abuse

I moved from friend's house to friend's house, staying a month here, a month there, a night or two at a hotel in between. And there was always my mum and dad's. That was until my nan died and my mum inherited some money. So they left London for Dartford in Kent and my brother bought the family home in Battersea on the understanding that I could live there rent-free, until such a time when I didn't need to and then he could do what he wanted with it. My parents basically gave me the house to live in because I was homeless – there was no point giving me cash because I couldn't be trusted with money.

I turned the house into the biggest drug den ever. I moved one dealer into one bedroom and another into the other. My mum still had a really annoying habit of popping round to check on me unannounced, which fucked me off no end, but by this stage she was worried sick about me. Anyway, she turned up at the house which, by then, I'd run into the ground. I remember it was a Tuesday because I was irritated that she'd come up on a Tuesday. I mean, why the fuck was she coming to see me on a Tuesday? She knew that was the day of the fucking dead. Me and my mum were sat on this cream leather sofa next to this massive fish tank, which had been a present from my dad. It had basically been too big for them to take with them so – surprise – it was left for me as a gift. And I remember saying to her, 'I've got something I have to tell you. Something I haven't told anyone,' I said. 'Mum, I was sexually abused when I was a kid.'

I don't know why I chose that day to tell her. It had been eating away at me for a long, long time. I'd just lost Tom, and it had made me look at my life and the things that needed to be said, and I just knew I had to tell her. I think I'd been looking for excuses for why I was this awful person, too, and if I could blame it on the fact that I'd been sexually abused, that might help.

The main reason I hadn't ever spoken about it before was, I think, because I was a gay child. I had no doubt about my sexuality when I was growing up and I never felt I had to come out – I was always out. But somehow I had come to think – wrongly – that the abuse I experienced as a boy was a part of growing up gay – maybe that was what just happened to gay kids, you know? There was no handbook to consult, there was no *My First Dick*, '74 edition. But my abuser had also made me believe that if I ever told anyone, I would be the one in trouble. He made me believe that I had instigated it, that I was the perpetrator, not him, and that it was all my fault. Even now, even though I know it wasn't me, I still hate to talk about it – even in therapy. But it explains a lot of my early sexual experiences, it shaped my relationship with sex, which in turn shaped my relationships with partners. And it also explains a lot of the psychology that shaped my addiction. What happened to me is part of my story, so here you go.

In the summer holidays, I used to go to an arts centre just up the road. It's still there now and is a community project which offers drama workshops, art classes and youth clubs, that sort of thing. I probably started going there when I was about ten or so. I was the only one out of my brothers to go – Kevin was always in trouble with the police and Dean was too young. They wouldn't have gone there anyway, to be honest, but being a child on my own did make it easier to single me out.

One of the activities they had there was a Friday night film club. They would show the most recent films that had come out – things like *Jaws* and shit like that, and the club was run by a guy who I'll call JB. To me at the time, he seemed really old, but when I look back at it now he was probably only in his thirties. He had this horrible combover hair, wore big thick black-rimmed glasses, and had these awful lips that were always wet. Urgh, they were awful. There was a smell about him too, an unwashed, musty smell, like clothes that have been stuck in the wardrobe too long. He wore cheap suits and he had a tacky black pleather jacket with a fur collar. If basic-bitch had been a thing back then he most definitely would have been the epitome.

JB quickly befriended me and would chat to me at the film club, asking me about myself and my family. My mum was ill at the time and my dad was doing everything he could to keep everything together, so there wasn't a whole lot of attention going around at home. It was nice suddenly having someone just focussing on me. He started by asking if I needed money and offered me a Saturday job working at the odd thing with him. And you know, that in itself was quite a big thing. I didn't come from a family with loads of money, and someone was actually offering me a job. I think he had cottoned on to the fact that I was gay. It wasn't like I was going down there and running around in drag – I was just a kid – but I was still me. Anyway, he'd sussed me out and over the course of the coming weeks I'd see him at the arts centre and he kept saying, 'If you want to earn some money then come and work for me.'

It didn't take long – just a couple of months of going along to his film club each week – before I agreed to take the job as his Saturday assistant. I would sit there and watch the projector while he went off to do another job. I forget exactly how much I used to get paid but I remember him giving me twenty quid once. I don't think that was the usual amount – I think that was more as a sweetener at the beginning. It was all very odd really, but my mum was in and out of hospital, and with my dad working flat out there was a lot going on, and I guess he saw a situation that he could take advantage of and went for it.

He built up trust with my parents and made them believe that I was safe with him. With them he was the nicest person on the planet – he came to the house when he first offered me the job to talk it through with them and made out that getting me involved with showing films would help me become an actor. They were thrilled that someone was giving me a job and helping me too, and if that had been the truth, it would have been great. My mum would never have allowed me to be in a situation if she'd known for one second that anything was going on. But he manipulated everything that was going on with my family at the time and I think my parents were just so happy that I had something to take me out of our home environment for a bit.

I can't remember exactly how the abuse started, but the first thing that really sticks out in my mind was him asking me to stand behind him and put my hands into his trouser pockets. I remember feeling physically sick, I was absolutely repulsed, and I was scared. I'd had an awareness of the situation gradually changing, him coming into close physical contact with me when he didn't need to, his hand brushing over me, and I was terrified that this was now happening. Even now thinking about it makes me feel sick. I remember him having nylon pocket lining, he had an erection and made me feel it. He was wearing a Prince of Wales check suit. It still makes me shudder just thinking of it.

It just progressed from there. I suppose now you would say he groomed me. He was paying me as his assistant and his previous assistant – the boy before me – was still getting money out of him, so I think it must have been a pattern. I deeply regret not telling anyone at the time because there must have been a whole list of boys before me, and I'm sure there was a list of boys after me who, if I'd spoken out, I might have been able to stop. But he made it so I couldn't tell anyone. He'd say to me, 'If you tell anyone I'll say that you were the one that started all of this. You were the one who put your hands in my pockets.' He made me believe that I was the one who had actually brought it on myself. And I was just a ten-year-old kid, a kid coming to terms with his sexuality, which he preyed on. It was all I could do to push it to one side to deal with it at the time. I had loads of friends at the arts centre but none of them picked up on it, and because when I was with him and not with my friends, he would isolate me. My mum was really ill and even if I'd wanted to, I didn't think I could burden her with anything at the time, he made me feel disgusted with myself. He was paying me and in my head I wasn't sure what he was paying me for . . . was he paying me for *that*? Was that a part of the transaction? I was accepting his cash, so how could I speak out about it?

You have to remember, with abusers and paedophiles, it's not a spur-of-the-moment thing they do, it's manipulative and carefully calculated. They're predators and they know how to catch their prey. That's their life. It's not just a one-off situation that happened to happen, that's what that guy had been doing all of his adult life. You might have thought that the other staff at the arts centre would have noticed what was going on, but he picked his moments and made sure that no one spotted him doing anything. With abusers, they know what they're doing, and they know how to use their position of power and trust. It was all very twisted and warped and I was made to feel like I was the one in the wrong.

It wasn't long before he put pressure on me to do other things, things that I really didn't want to do. It progressed from him getting me to put my hands in his pockets to him getting me to wank him off, which seemed so alien to me. How it led to that is a little blurry, but as it progressed he'd make up reasons for me to spend more time with him. He would tell my mum and dad that he had a job working away somewhere – say Birmingham or somewhere like that – and that we would need to stay overnight at a guesthouse before driving back. So I would go away with him and he'd have me for the night, but we never actually went anywhere. My family lived in Lavender Hill, just near Clapham Junction, and we would stay less than a mile away in a guest house in Battersea Rise. I'd have to lie to my parents that we'd been away, I can't tell you why I did, just that I really had been made to believe that if it all came out, I would be the one in trouble. Now, when I think about it, I wonder if the woman who ran the guesthouse was in on it, too. He would tell people that he was my uncle, and it wasn't like we slept in a double bed, but still. It was 1975 and a very different time, but when I look back at it, it was all clearly so very wrong.

He had a caravan in Canvey Island, near Leigh-on-Sea. It was grim as fuck and he'd take me down there in the middle of winter under the guise of it needing to be painted, a 'job' he was paying me to help him with. Nothing would be open on the caravan site and he definitely wasn't going there for the crazy golf. It was the most decrepit, hideous old thing that smelt of mould and damp with a pull-down bed. I can still recall those smells now when I think of it. He built up from taking me away for a night, up to a weekend. I was scared, he was blackmailing me and saying that I instigated it all, and I'd just want to get back home. Then he took me on holiday with him to Lloret de Mar, in Spain. Let's be clear here – it was no holiday. It was a trip . . . I wasn't there making sandcastles. Fuck knows how he was even allowed to take me out of the country – that just wouldn't happen now. He told my mum that he was taking all of the staff away with him and that it wasn't just the two of us. And this is where it gets murky in my mind. I hated him but I really wanted to go on a plane – I'd never been on one before. So was the trip my fault too? By this point I absolutely detested him and was stealing money from him, so I thought, *Why not, I'll take a free flight and a trip from you.* I remember being there in Spain and this woman said to me, 'That's not your uncle, is it? You can talk to us you know.' And another time being on the beach and this guy saying to me, 'If that's not your uncle and you need to talk then you can tell me.' But I just denied it every time. I must have been twelve or thirteen by that stage, I was protecting him to protect myself. I didn't know what was going to happen if the truth came out.

In my twelve-year-old head, it was all skewed. He was paying me to be his assistant and made me believe it was a part of the job, that I was being paid for one thing and so was being paid for the other, too. But I hated him, and it made me hate who I was. I remember the first time I ejaculated when I was with him, and he was a bit like, 'Oh my God, you ejaculated.' I think he liked really young boys, it wasn't like a teenage thing. There was never any actual penetrative sex – for him it was more the touching and that kind of thing, but that doesn't change how damaging and abusive the situation was. It was vile. He would probably instigate a situation where he could have sex with me about once a week, but then when we went away it was all the time. I remember he would make me suck his dick and there would always be fluff in his belly button, even now I can recall the image of it, over forty years later, and when I do, it makes me feel sick.

He never threatened me physically but there was a lot of mental torture. It was really fucking twisted. But I was just a kid, and all I knew was to bottle it all up. I think my mum would pick up on things sometimes, would sense that my mood was off. She'd ask me what was wrong and I'd just say I'd had an argument with him or make something up. I just didn't feel like I could put it on her when she was so sick. I couldn't go to my dad and tell him either because he would have murdered the man. And also, because I knew I was gay, I kind of believed that I had brought it on. That was what JB made me believe – that I had instigated it all. That it was my fault. The abuse had forced a kind of early sexualisation and my awareness of being 'different', of being gay, somehow meant the two became entwined – being gay and the abuse, I couldn't tell them apart. I was still a kid, and that's just how it went.

At that time, I had decided that I wanted to be an actor. Of course I did. I told JB and about a year in, he said he knew a guy in the film industry and took me to meet him at a place on Wardour Street. At that time, that was the capital of film in England, and all of the film companies would have offices there. I remember going to see this guy called Hugh. He had grey hair and wore thick black-rimmed glasses too and, of course, was another paedophile. I remember wondering if they all wore the same glasses. I don't know if it was a paedophile ring or not, but I don't know how they would have found each other if it wasn't. We went to Wardour Street and met this men and then he invited us to his house for the weekend. To me, it seemed like the country, but it could just as easily have been Acton. There was just the three of us in this cottage, another point where I think, *How on earth was he allowed to do that and take me there?* When we were there they showed me porn. I don't remember it, I think I just switched off. This was before VHS, so they showed it on a big screen in the house on a projector. It was old porn films, which I think they had made, and which included young boys. They'd tried everything they could to get me to have sex with them and I could tell they were aroused, but somehow I managed to avoid it. I can't remember how. The detail around some of this stuff is really cloudy. I think when things get so bad, you learn to block it out.

By the time I went to secondary school I was making myself ill all of the time. The first time was a genuine accident, I fell off my skateboard and cracked my head open, but it made me realise that it was a good way to make myself unavailable to him. I think me being on crutches all that time and going back and forth to hospital was a big part of me avoiding him. He came to visit me in hospital once and brought me a present. It was one of those old handheld computer games – just some lines on the screen that you'd move left and right and play bat and ball, which went 'beep, beep'. I remember him saying, 'Come with me and let me touch you in the toilets,' and I was like, 'Fuck off – I'm in hospital.' That's how twisted he was. Me getting fat was perhaps another way for me to put a barrier around myself. It's not like I planned to put on weight, but food became a comfort. I was eating to change the way I felt, and I started to put on weight. And then that became a kind of protection. I didn't know any other way of escaping.

To this day I can't remember how it ended with JB. I've thought about it a lot and talked to counsellors about it in preparation for writing this, but it's a blank. I know I'd started to try and make more and more reasons not to see him, but in reality I think a big part of it was that I just got too old for him. I was well into adolescence by that point and, like I said, he liked young boys. Sadly, he probably moved on to the next kid, and then the next. Just like I'm sure there had been a long list of boys before me. I wish I'd spoken out as a child, but I think as a twelve-year-old, you're just trying to deal with it.

I think maybe the last time I saw him, he came to pick me up for work from my house. It was a Friday night, and that week I'd bleached my hair and had tramlines cut in. I told him to fuck off and that I wasn't going with him. I don't think he liked the fact that I had started thinking and speaking for myself. Those four years of growing from a ten-year-old boy to a fourteen-year-old kid, all the time being abused by him, meant that he'd effectively ended my childhood.

When I did finally tell my mum that day, all those years later, I'll never forget the look on her face and the pain in her eyes from what I'd just told her. I remember her starting to cry and just wanting to hold me, and she kept repeating, 'I'm so sorry, I'm so sorry, I should have known.' I think we were probably together for another few hours after that, going over the 'coulda, woulda, shouldas' of it all. She felt she should have spotted it, noticed some signs. But how could she have known? There was never a moment when I blamed her for not working it out, because I covered it up and kept it from them. There was only ever one person to blame, and that was him. But I do remember feeling a huge sense of relief when I told her. The only person I'd ever told before that was my friend Gabby who I went to Ibiza with. We still decided not to tell my dad though – he would have gone mental, not at me, but knowing someone had done that to his son – and we decided it was best if he never knew. If I'm honest, I think part of me telling her had been purely for selfish reasons – I was in the middle of my addiction, I was a fucking mess, I was trying to cover up that I was killing myself and that I was dying of HIV. The abuse was my absolute trump card, but I also believe that it came out of my mouth at that time because it needed to. It had needed to come out for a very, very long time.

The abuse sexualised me, it changed the way I felt. I was made to feel dirty, I was made to feel unlovable, I was made to feel worthless, I felt trapped by shame. But I realised there was a way I could use what I had to control men – or at least that's how I chose to see it. By the time I went to secondary school, I'd be leaving class and going cottaging in the park. Because that's what people – or gay men – did then. They didn't have Grindr or social media to hook up with people. That's how they met. I was too young even by my standards to go out to bars and clubs. But I had normalised casual and random sex with strangers and would have blow jobs with as many people as I could in a day, sometimes it could be up to ten. But that's the way the abuse had affected me and it would take years for me to even start to work through it.

For those reading this who are straight or who have never been cruising, you would go somewhere that you knew was a cruising spot – like the toilets in Battersea Park – hang around and wait for someone to make eye contact with you. It was as easy as that. You both knew what you were there for. You would stumble across cruising spots because in the dark days, before hook-up apps and homosexuality being so openly accepted, men would write messages on the walls and toilet doors, and you'd just come across them, quite innocently, by using the toilets. The thing with casual, anonymous sex is that it might be a fantasy for some, a desire, but every time you do it, it chips a little bit more away from you until you have nothing but a void of self-hatred. The cruising was always sex in toilets or in the park, or up on the roof of the pump house in Battersea Park, which at the time was derelict but which is now a picture gallery – and you would have to climb to get to it. It was actually really dangerous. I mean, what a way that would have been to kill yourself – getting a blow job on a roof. Every time I walk past it now, walking the dog, whoever I'm with, I tell them the same story.

Another sexual watershed moment from my early teens was me instigating sex with the teacher at school which, you'll remember, is how I eventually got expelled. I saw myself as some kind of gay femme fatale that had this super-power over men. Drama had been the only class I really enjoyed and attended, so I would orchestrate these situations where I did extra drama class after school or went to see him for advice. To this day, I don't believe the teacher was an abuser. I put the pressure on and I was just so confused by who and what I was and what I felt, that sex was my only bargaining tool. It was my new thing. I was fifteen, my hormones were raging and I had become equipped – rightly or wrongly – with the know-how to get what I wanted.

There was this guy who lived in Battersea Park Mansions who I'd met cruising in the park. He said to me, 'Ooh, you could make a lot of money with a dick like that.' I thought he wanted me to do porn or be my pimp or something, but he told me about the Meat Rack in Soho where you could pick up men for money. You would stand at the top of the stairs, where NatWest is now, and someone would come up to you and ask if you were free, then you'd go off down an alley or back to their house. It would never be for more than an hour, sometimes you could be in and out in fifteen minutes, so it wasn't a hard thing to cover up. It wasn't like I was missing for hours and anyone was wondering where I was.

There was a whole gang of rent boys and you had to be careful as you were on their patch, so I went on Sunday mornings. The thing was, I was so confused about having been given money by JB and feeling like I had been paid for sex that it had become almost normalised for me. I can't remember when it started – I think I must have been about fifteen – and looking back, it was an awful but, in many ways, obvious progression from what I'd already experienced. I simply took it to the next level. I'd go back to their flat or house and I would absolutely hate them and then take their ten quid for it.

I was such a little skank. I used to nick stuff from their houses and give it to people. I thought I was the Robin Hood of the Meat Rack. Stealing from the rich and giving to the poor. I'd lift it whilst I was there and give it to my mates on the estate – sovereign rings and bracelets, that kind of stuff. People used to ask me where I'd got it from and I'd say that I'd found it. I would never admit that I'd found it in some man's bathroom. I thought I was teaching them a lesson. I remember stealing this married man's wedding rings and about a week later him coming after me and being like 'I need them back, my wife's asking me what's happened to them.' And I had to go back and get them from the people I'd given them away to.

Even when I had been working on the King's Road, I'd sometimes go back to Piccadilly to earn a bit of extra money. Weirdly, I was never scared when I was doing it. I think I'd been through so much by that point that I wasn't scared of anything. None of the sex I ever had at this time was penetrative – for some reason that feels important to say. That came later when I started going clubbing at sixteen.

The first time I did it was with Roy from the Embassy Club, he passed me a bottle of poppers and said, 'Here, sniff these – you'll be able to get a kitchen table up there afterward.' And you know what, he was fucking right.

THINGS I LEARNED FROM MY MUM

Never to shut up.

I learned how to stand up for myself.

I learned how to spend vast amounts of money under the
radar without anyone knowing.

I learned freedom. My mum allowed me to have permed hair,
my mum really allowed me to live in the skin I was in. She
allowed me the freedom to be in drag at fourteen. She just
let me be who I am.

I learned the skill of being in the wrong but
always being right.

I learned how to stand by someone unconditionally
and support them.

I learned how to sneak new clothes and shoes into the
house without your partner knowing.

I learned to never give up on people.

I learned never to take requests.

11.

No K, No Play

You should always be careful what shit you put out there at the height of your career, because you never know when it's going to come back and haunt you. I was booked by Donatella Versace to play a private after-party in her Milan penthouse a few years ago – it was the show where Jennifer Lopez had come back to model a version of the green print dress she originally wore in 2000. Anyway, in walks Donatella, arm in arm with J-Lo, I'm behind the decks with as much Versace bling on as I can lift, and she goes 'Aiii, Fat Tony! NO K, NO PLAY!!' I mean, fuck me. How the fuck did she know that?

I mean, when you think about it, you could say that I was one of the early pioneers of crowdsourcing – I was the club equivalent of GoFundMe, a real life, real time, 'Drugs for Tony' ket-raising campaign. I would turn the music off on the main dance floor and shout out 'No K, No Play' and not put the music on until someone had brought me some drugs. I thought I was being really fucking clever.

Our weekends at that stage, around 1999–2000, were very much on a schedule – well, as much of a schedule as a bunch of idiotic, car-crash, drug-addict junkies can muster. I would play Milk Bar or somewhere in Soho on the Friday night and then go to someone's house or a club called the Viaduct. I mean, we would go anywhere until the Saturday night, and then it would be everyone down to Trade. After Trade, we would go to DTPM, which at that time was at Villa Stefano in Holborn. Trade's music was predominantly hardcore techno and hard house, which basically was shit house. They started to do this 'light' room at Trade, which was run by these two DJ's called the Sharp Boys, and of course, the little cuckoo that I am, I infiltrated and took it over in a matter of months and it became the most popular of the rooms. People really began to like that soulfully disco-defected type sound of house music. I mean, you could dance to it for a start, rather than just standing there gurning your face off.

By the time I got to Trade to do my set at 10am on a Sunday morning, having played at Milk Bar and places like that, I would have been to a few after-parties and not slept for two days. I would be about to play an eight-hour set completely off my nut. I mean, Jesus fucking Christ. I would stop the music and say, 'Right, I want drugs. Someone get me some drugs.' It was a part of the persona that I was wheeling around town at the time, the Tony car crash. It was the early noughties – DJ's were expected to behave badly. That's what I told myself, anyway.

Gina would be in there all the time and I remember us both sitting there, me off my nut on ketamine and him in full Boy George persona mode, he flicked his hand at me making some bitchy queen comment and this massive diamond cluster ring flew off his finger and across the room. We must have spent fucking hours looking for it but he was so tired that he was just like, 'Forget about it, don't worry.' I was clearing out my record box four months later and found it at the bottom. Amazingly, and very unlike me at the time, I called and told him I'd found it. I'm surprised I didn't take it and try to trade it for a few eight-balls. Anyway, that was how 'No K, No Play' came about. I'd turn the music off, people would be like, 'Shit, quick – get some drugs for Tony,' and they would bring drugs to the DJ box, offer me a line or a few bumps, and off we'd go. I'd start the music again. After a while it became this huge thing on the club scene when I did a set, and people would just bring me anything I wanted.

This was when Trade was at Turnmills, in Farringdon. It was around the late 90s, and it was insane. Trade was amazing because it was our playground, you could literally do whatever the fuck you wanted. And we really did. I've never been to any place like it, ever. People talk about the Berghain now, but it's not the same – as free as it is, it's all controlled. Trade never was. It was literally a free-for-all. You would have queues of people lining up to buy pills. Forty people all standing there waiting, like they were in the queue for the Post Office. Upstairs in the toilets there would be six people per cubicle having sex. You couldn't make it up, and of course for someone like me with my addictive personality, it was like heaven on earth, and I was being paid to be there. I was getting smoke blown up my arse, both literally and figuratively.

It was only when the council tried to shut Turnmills down and it got raided that it stopped being quite so uninhibited. But until then, it was a Friday night at the Gallery, and then Saturday morning at Gallery, then it would roll into Sunday, then Sunday night, which led all the way through to Monday afternoon. It was pure chaos, hot and sweaty in there, it really was the last of those old-school nightclubs. But these things have their natural life cycle, they grow, and become massive and then they die – like anything, it had a sell-by date.

I had a solid clubbing crew at this point – Stratty, Lisa and Edna – and they were like family. They came with me everywhere, along with my long-suffering boyfriend Johnny, who I put through absolute hell. I met Stratty out clubbing at Trade and we just started hanging out together. We were so on each other's wavelength – he loved to take the piss and laugh and, most importantly, he really fucking loved drugs. I think the first thing he said to me was to ask where he could get coke from. Stratty was from Coventry and he was the closest you could get to Dickensian London – he would smile at you whilst he had his hand in your pocket stealing your wallet. He was one of those people that just did not give a shit and he fitted in perfectly. He was into Buddhism whilst snorting cocaine off toilet seats. For every wrong in Stratty, there was a right, and that's what gave him his magic. You would see him and you'd just laugh. He looked like The Penguin from *Batman* and was just the funniest person on the planet. He earned the right to be my best friend very quickly. Because we were on the mission . . . Stratty would walk into the room and light it up. You knew that, if something went missing at a party, it was Stratty, if there was trouble at a party, it was Stratty, but he was one of the most loyal people on the planet. He was always in borrowed clothes – everything he wore would have been found in lost property, every picture I have of him in my phone, he's dressed in my clothes. He'd sit there in my Adidas jacket and be like, 'Guurl, can I wear this?' And I'd always be like, 'Yeah, but

I want it back.' You would never see it again. He's the same now – I sometimes see him walking around Battersea. He never got clean. I'll sit and talk to him and I look at him and think, *Wow, that was me twenty years ago.*

Lisa was the girlfriend of one of the bouncers at Trade. He brought her up to me and said, 'My girlfriend wants to meet you.' And there she was, all the way from Barnet, with serious attitude. No one could sneer like her, but you know, you wait a lifetime for a Lisa. Because Lisa's another one, a friend for life and she's everything. Well, apart from the fact that she comes from Barnet. When people tell me I'm only friends with famous people, they can fuck off, because my friends come from all walks of life. When I first met Lisa, she thought she was really glamorous – I mean, she was. It was the end of the 90s, and the era of the bootcut jean and boob tube, and she loved that look, and she loved a good time. She was always starting trouble in clubs and would always be going out with a tough guy who would end up fighting for her. If you had an argument with Lisa you'd better make sure there were no ashtrays around because you'd get one thrown at your head. We used to fight like brother and sister, we were awful. She'd say things like: 'Where've you been? Look at the state of ya.' I remember us going to my nephew's christening and me turning up gurning, and she was like, 'Look at the fucking state of you, you've ruined your brother's day,' and I'd be like, 'You can talk, look at the state of you, ya fat bitch'. But she's stuck with me through thick and thin.

Edna's nickname was Rat Skin when we first met him, I'm not sure why. His real name was Mark McKenzie and he did so much fucking speed that you would talk to him and he would tell you about sixteen different stories all at the same time, all in the same sentence. We thought that the name Edna suited him much better. He had a sweet magic about him – he was like a stray dog; you stroked him, you showed him a bit of love, and he would be your best friend. And you know what, everyone needs an Edna in their life. He was a fixer and has one of the most creative minds; you can just see it always ticking over. He did all the artwork inside of Trade, he was a genius. When he was on speed it was like a little gay Speedy Gonzalez, zoom, zoom, zoom. Edna always had been and always will be a force of nature.

He, Stratty and Lisa were all cut from the same cloth. You would see them and they'd have been up for four days and were just trouble. They'd come to your house and would never fucking leave. They would literally wear every item from your wardrobe over each other as drag and hang out the window screaming.

Incredibly, I still looked good up until the 'No K, No Play' years. The drugs had taken over to the extent that I was rail-thin, but that was no bad thing in my book. I had tiger-striped hair and dressed in Fake London jeans, Tom Ford-era Gucci shirt, and Patrick Cox Wannabe shoes. The drugs hadn't completely ravished me yet – I'd say this was the very last point before it really went downhill. I was still a major drug addict but you wouldn't look at me and think that I'd just been pulled from a gutter on the street.

The change during that time, 1996–7, was pretty dramatic. It was right in the middle of the 'No K, No Play' years and I looked my absolute worst. There's a picture I always put up on Instagram – it's in this book too – when I'm celebrating my clean time birthday. It is like a picture of death warmed up, I look like I'm sitting in God's waiting room.

I had tipped over the point of being a functional addict to being completely lost in it.

As much of a mess as I was at that stage, I would still make it to every gig. There must have been a few times when I didn't show up at the right time but this was how I made my drug money so whatever state I was in, I would always make it. I would stumble in and somehow play. Reliable old Tony. What a fucking trooper.

The weekend just wouldn't stop. We'd always have to find somewhere else to go and create a new night somewhere. We went through a phase of going to the pubs in Smithfield Meat Market. It was the perfect way to carry on the weekend because the pubs would open at 2am so that the butchers working the nightshift on the market could get a pint when they finished. We found this pub and infiltrated it, side by side with all the fucking butchers, coked off our nuts on what was by now a Monday morning.

One time we went there, I thought everyone was completely covered in blood – everyone was wearing white and seemed to be dripping in the stuff. I was tripping my tits off. Another time, it was a Monday lunchtime and all my cronies had gone. I sat in the corner with the newspaper and the whole pub seemed to be staring at me. I sat there for about two hours, unable to move, and desperate to go to the toilet. I thought that if I as much as looked up from the paper, they would all realise I was definitely off my nut. I felt completely delirious. For hours I sat there not daring to move, completely pranged off my nut, and they weren't fucking staring at me at all. They were watching the football on TV. I was sat underneath the screen. What an idiot.

I was completely hooked on downers: Rohypnol,

temazepam, diazepam – my absolute favourites were liquid diazepam. Oooh, they were delicious. They came in these tiny little tubes, or in a little square pouch that you would rip open, and they would hit you straight away. The best way to get the strongest hit from them was to do them up your arse. The amount of straight mates I would end up doing Rohypnol with was unreal. They would call me up and be like, 'Oh, we've got these – do you want to come over?' I'd be like, 'All right, I'm on my way!' and we'd squirt liquid diazepam up each other's bums. Now you'd look at it and think it was a fucking weird situation, but then what was a 'normal' situation from my life at the time?

I was such a tight fucker when it came to drugs. If I was being offered your drugs, then great, but if they were my drugs, they were never being offered to anyone, ever. You're having a laugh, ain't you? Do your drugs and I'll do my drugs, and if you've got any left then I'll do your drugs too. But I would never, ever, ever give any drugs away.

We soon got bored of Smithfield Market and instead found these two old queens who were running a leather bar in the Prince of Orange pub over in Rotherhithe. You'd shout through the letterbox and they'd let you in and they had all of these sex mazes upstairs and they started this after-hours club which had banging techno. Anyway, we decided it was going to be THE new after-hours club on the Monday morning, and the fact that it was a leather bar made it that much cooler. Within weeks I was DJ'ing there and we called it 'The Orange'. It started off as ten of us, then it would be twenty of us and then thirty or forty of us, and it just became the place to be. Honestly, there was so much dry ice and smoke in there you could only see about a foot in front of your face. It was so debauched. I remember it got raided once by the police. We had these strobe lights on and I released so much dry ice we could all run out through the back door. Sometimes I used to get electrocuted behind the DJ box – there was water all over the floor and wires going into it. It was basic as fuck!

That's when we started selling 'No FT, No Coke' and 'No Coke, No FT' T-shirts. Lisa, Stratty and Graham, who was my ketamine dealer and who I'd moved into one of the bedrooms at the house in Battersea. They came up with them one night when they were off their heads, and I got really ill and went into hospital with my HIV diagnosis. Off they went and got a load of T-shirts printed and went around the clubs selling them, the aim being to raise enough money to send me on holiday when I got out. Lisa was in charge of finances, which was the worst idea ever. I never saw a penny of the money, but it was a very sweet, enterprising idea. If it had been the other way round I don't think they would have seen a penny of it either, to be honest.

It was about then that my teeth started to go. All the coke over the years had made my gums recede and itch, and hurt, then I'd be rubbing even more coke onto them, which made them even worse. I got an infection in my mouth and it went septic, and at that stage my HIV was so bad that my body just couldn't fight off infection. That was when I started digging at the teeth with my fingers because I just couldn't bear the feeling in my gums, and it became obsessive. I'd always chewed my nails and put my fingers in my mouth and me picking at my teeth became the next level – and God knows what was on my fingers. Then crystal meth came along and the intensity of that drug was so insane – and this is bearing in mind that I'd been freebasing eight-balls of cocaine for years – that it just sent me over the edge. My brain couldn't deal with it.

I think that was when the real turning point in my self-destruction came. It was then that I thought to myself, *Well, this is who I am now so I just need to accept it. I'm a fucking mess and this is my future.* It wasn't a good place to be.

I got what they call 'meth mouth', where my gums were so dehydrated and full of bacteria that I actually thought I had animals and bugs living in them. That's when I really started working on my teeth, fiddling with them and using anything I had to hand to just give any kind of release – scissors, screwdrivers, kitchen knives, anything.

I remember the first time that I lost a tooth. I was at Orange at The Viaduct and my front tooth fell out. It was my front right tooth, and I could feel the air coming into my mouth; it was such a shock. I carried on DJ'ing and made a joke, but it shocked me. Then from there the next tooth would rot and fall out. All I did was drink whisky and Coca-Cola and do cocaine and crystal meth. And I'd just tug and pull at them because they'd be hurting so much and one by one they'd fall out. They weren't nice teeth by that point, they were totally drug-fucked teeth, and I just wanted them out of my head. My face was so numb a lot of the time with the drugs I was doing that I'd be able to pull a tooth out without realising how excruciating it was. It wouldn't be until the next day that I would wake up in throbbing agony with another infection and have to go to hospital and be pumped with yet another round of antibiotics.

There's so much shame attached to your teeth in our society – bad teeth and you're poor, terrible teeth and you're a junkie, or you live on the streets or you haven't looked after yourself. Well, I was a bit of all three by that point and I was so ashamed that it never even came into my mind that I should see a dentist. When you see homeless people doing drinks or drugs on the street, and you think, 'How can they get into that state? Look at them.' I know how you can get into that state. I've been in that state. That state becomes the norm, because that's what you feel you deserve. It's a fucking awful place to be.

Aside from my gorgeous teeth, I also stank like a dead dog. I remember being on the bus once with Stratty, sitting at the back, and people were getting up and moving to the front because we stank so much . . . The thing with heavy drug users, if you're not familiar, is that the drugs have to come out somewhere. Mine came out in my feet and in my scalp. Some people have them come out through their hands, some get sweaty faces. Methadone and ketamine make people smell quite chemical. My drugs would come out through my feet – I would take my socks off and they would stand up on their own. And that was just the socks. My actual feet were even worse, they would boggle your mind. They would be white and withered from sweat, the skin shrivelled up like when you've been in the bath too long, bits of sludge stuck in my nails, they were shitting drugs and the stench was unbelievable, but I was obsessed with the smell of it.

I should say that by now I was 100% mentally ill. At one stage I had a septic finger and it wouldn't get any better – I didn't have the immune system to fight off infection, but also I kept pulling the plaster I had on it back, smelling the rank infection and then putting the plaster back on. I was obsessed with the smell of the rotting flesh. It would get better and then I would have a good old poke at it and

I would reinfect it. I mean, who cultivates a septic finger like it's a pet? Do you know what I mean? I treated my septic finger like I had a cat, I was obsessed by it. It really wasn't normal behaviour.

Good news, though, you'll be pleased to hear I was still managing to have sex. Non-stop. Seriously, I could leave the flat to go and buy a packet of fags, with one tooth in my mouth and smelling like the dead, and still be able to pick up on the way back home.

I was like one of those filthy fucking alley cats spraying pheromones all the way to Tesco's and back.

THINGS YOU SHOULD NEVER SAY TO A DJ

Have you got any R&B?

Do you do requests?

Have you got a microphone? No. Fuck off, you cunt.

Do you know where the toilets are?

Can I have two sambucas and a pint of lager?

Yo mate, you look like you're off your nut – do you know
anyone selling any drugs?

Your music's shit.

Are you Danny Tenaglia?

'Scuse me, mate. What time's the next DJ on?

I thought you were dead.

Why are you called Fat Tony? You're not even fat.

'Scuse me, my mate's a DJ – do you mind if he goes on and
plays a couple of tunes?

12.
The End

Friday 1 December 2001

There were still a few people booking the Tony show, some out of loyalty, in the hope that I might manage to keep it together if I knew I had to turn up to a gig, some because they knew that people would turn up to watch the car crash. And so I was sitting in the back room of The Cross club waiting to DJ after nearly a week-long bender. I was like a zombie, the lights were out and I was rocking back and forth, wringing my hands and chewing my gums. My friend Edna ran in to tell me that my boyfriend Johnny was there. Our relationship by that point was as turbulent and toxic as they come. I'd cheated on him with pretty much every guy in London and as a result, most of our interactions now were physical – there wouldn't be black eyes but there was so much anger there that I just remember thinking, Christ, I can't fucking deal with this right now. *I was just about holding it together. I'd gone back to the flat earlier in the day and taken his Fake London jeans without asking and thought he was coming to drag them off my legs. I just couldn't deal with it.*

My whole body froze as he came in, literally every muscle tensed, the very last reserves of any senses I had were saying I was in for a fight. Johnny stopped and looked me up and down, his eyes full of sadness and a softness I hadn't seen for a long time. 'Tony, are you all right?' he said, and the kindness threw me. Then he said it again: 'Are you all right?' 'What?' I mumbled. I felt like all the walls were closing in around me, rushing towards me and down on me in waves. 'What happened to you, Tony? Where did you go?' And something broke, deep inside. I started crying, huge, overpowering, chest-heaving, body-shaking sobs, and they wouldn't stop. Please, get me out of here.

Even though it might sound like it was the end, the incident at The Cross was in fact my lightbulb moment. You might read it as a breakdown, but it wasn't. The breakdown had happened ten years earlier. The Cross was the moment the pilot light was relit, when the gas went back on and a little bit of life came back to me. It wasn't a moment of 'I can't carry on anymore, I have to end it,' it was a moment of 'I can't carry on anymore, something has to change.'

That was the Friday night, I left the club straight away – crying – with Johnny. We went home and Johnny stayed with me all weekend and that Monday morning I went to the doctor and admitted I couldn't stop and that I needed help. I'd first met Johnny in a club about nine years earlier. When I met him he had a face like an angel, honestly he looked like a gift from God. I saw him and my head just spun, you know when you meet someone and you're like 'Oh my God, who is that boy?' He's still a very handsome man now. But when I saw him I just thought, *I want to spend the rest of my life with you.* He had a scar on his right cheek and he was everything – he was mouthy, he was trouble personified and I was just drawn to him. I asked if I could use his phone to make a call and went outside and stole it. He kept calling me to try and get it back and I just said, 'If you want your phone back you've got to come and meet me.' He came out to find me, and we just kind of started a relationship. He wasn't out then so there was always this kind of edginess to him, which I obviously loved. He was eighteen when I met him. Blonde with bright blue eyes, wrapped in a Burberry scarf. He was like the Artful Dodger and Oliver rolled into one, with a real straight-lad, North London voice. Honestly, as soon as you looked at him and he opened his mouth to speak you were just like, *Oh my God, I want to be with you forever.*

My birthday had always been the perfect excuse for a big old bender, and the last one before I became sober was no exception. I'd already been out since the Wednesday, and it was one of those weeks where Johnny had had enough of me. I'd told him that he needn't bother to kick me out, that I was leaving anyway and flounced out. I remember thinking, *Fuck you*. I hid in a Portaloo next to some road-works near the flat, waited until Johnny had gone, broke into the flat, stole some of his clothes and went back out again. Ha. Fuck You!

By the Friday, I was so exhausted and so dehydrated that everything just hurt, even my bones. My mouth and my gums were on fire and if I stopped and sat down for any length of time I would just rock back and forth. Without any exaggeration, the next stop was death. Part of me just knew inside that I was so unwell I was going to die. The night before my birthday I'd been to a chill-out, which is very basically that – a chill-out. It's when all the clubs have closed and someone goes, 'Oh, we could go back to mine,' so you all traipse round to someone's house, finish off all your drugs and then wait for the drug dealers to wake up and start working again. All sorts can happen. I had a threesome with two random guys while off my nut – that's how I'd started my big day. It wasn't unusual at this stage for me to cheat on Johnny, we were as bad as each other, but really, this was the end of the very end. There was nowhere else to go.

I'd never been suicidal, and I thank God for that. My heart breaks for anyone who feels their soul has been truly broken and who just can't see any way out. But there is always another way, and even a broken soul can heal. I think the worst it ever got for me was when I moved back in with Johnny, after one of our many break-ups, and contemplated jumping off Vauxhall Bridge. I'd been out for about four days and was tripping badly. I'd come back in a state and he'd broken up with me (again) and I was throwing one of my big dramas and threatening to kill myself. I stormed out of the house and down to Vauxhall Bridge and sat there thinking about how I was going to jump. Then I decided I wanted a cigarette but they were at home, so I walked back to get the cigarettes, and by that point I kind of thought I may as well sleep on it and decide the next day. I'm not sure if that counts, to be honest. And I think that anyone who has ever been seriously suicidal, so low that they can't imagine any other way, would agree with me.

Because, no matter how dark my life and my situation has got, and believe me, at times it has been pitch black, I've still somehow clung on to changing something, working something out, or scamming my way to something, anything. You have to remember that, with addiction, I'd spent every day of the past twenty years trying to kill myself in some way – nothing was ever safe. Whether it was climbing through windows on the fourteenth floor of a tower block or pulling out my teeth, it was all about risk. Nothing had been casual – it was all casualty.

There hadn't been some big catalyst that suddenly made everything worse in the lead-up to all of this, there never is with addiction. I'd started a new after-hours gig at the Egg Club, which was just another way of us having somewhere to go. I think we started that in the summer but I couldn't tell you exactly when. We were such creatures of the night that we didn't really have seasons. Summer was annoying and an inconvenience – all that daylight and the heat made my feet stink.

Also, you didn't go on holiday. You couldn't travel. My life had got so small because the thing about addiction is that it keeps you with those people who are doing the same as you. You don't see anyone else, and you definitely don't travel. You don't travel because you can't keep it together to make it onto a flight and keep any sense of time or place. Mainly, you don't travel because you don't know if you're going to be able to get what you need when you get off the plane. When you're that reliant, it's too uncertain to risk going somewhere that you might not be able to get drugs.

I remember my last flight to America, having been up for two days at the Joiners Arms. I was wearing a leather Calvin Klein shirt and jeans with Gucci loafers that had holes in the soles, which I'd padded with pieces of cardboard and wrapped in gaffer tape. I went straight to the airport stinking of drugs and booze. I got a Burger King on my way through the terminal, just about made the flight and passed out in the toilets which the air hostess had to open manually so they could take off. I was still holding the

Burger King bag. What a class act. It didn't stop there, either. When I'd gone through security the other end they'd put red stickers on everything because I'd been such a mess and so I was pulled to one side and searched. The police found the gaffer-taped pads in my shoes and thought they were drugs packages that I was trying to smuggle. Luckily, I didn't have anything on me and they let me through, eventually. I had to lie through my teeth and pretend I was there to see a boyfriend and wasn't working.

I think that might have been the last time I went away before rehab, the last time that sticks in my memory, anyway. I remember being with my mates Lisa and Stratty – the holy fucking trinity – back at Stratty's squat one morning, which was a bit of a dank one-bedroom flat that was really badly kept and had shit everywhere. It must have been about 6am and I'd come up with some kind of 'off your tits, get rich quick' scam. Because by this point I'd lost any real money I'd earned and the cash I got from gigs went straight to the dealer. I remember always being a little relieved when we had no cash left and had exhausted every avenue so that we had to get anything on tick. When I didn't even have enough money for a packet of fags, that meant that we really had to stop. My plan was that if we could just get enough money together then we could use it to break the cycle and go on holiday. 'What are you talking about?' Stratty said. 'People like us don't go on holiday.' And I was like, 'You're right. People like us don't.'

Crystal meth hadn't been the start of my addiction, not by any stretch of the imagination, but it definitely accelerated the sprint to the end. I was hollow, there was nothing of me. I'd already lost a lot of weight, years before, but now

I was skeletal. Sometimes it still felt like we were having a good time. I'd hide under hats and glasses and I'd skulk around. I became very secretive. I'd swap groups of friends and would shake people off so that no one would know exactly what I'd done, or where I'd been. It's easier to take more, stay up longer and for no one to judge you if you shake off your original crew.

I would be at Trade and everyone would want me to play on and on and on, it was like my obsessive-compulsive disorder would override everything and I'd just play track after track after track. But to go on, I would need more drugs.

I remember being in the DJ box and Johnny came in. He was meant to be bringing more coke with him, and I'd been waiting for what felt like hours. He pulled this massive lump wrapped in clingfilm out of his pocket. It had sweated up in his pocket – if you're not familiar, that's when you keep coke somewhere warm and so it heats up and turns to a sticky mush, especially with crap coke that's been cut a lot. Anyway, he pulled it out of his pocket and held up what looked like a fruit pastel. I nearly burst into tears – the thought of him getting there with coke was the only thing keeping me going. What the fuck would I do now? I was at that point of exhaustion where I felt like I could collapse. I'd abused my body so much. I snatched the lump out of Johnny's hand mid-air, grabbed my Jack Daniels and Coke and swallowed the whole thing in one go before anyone could stop me. How that didn't kill me, considering I was seven stone and wet through at this stage, I'll never know.

I was quite open with everyone about my coke taking, and the ketamine. I was less forthcoming about the crystal meth, and the side-helping of Rohypnol. I would take any downers I could get my hands on by that stage, just to level me out and keep me from getting psychosis, which would normally start with paranoia and then could end with any scenario. I remember once thinking there were people all around me having a party and I was in a room on my own, and another time seeing people outside my house when there was no one there, or sitting in bed and eating soup from a bowl, neither of which were there. Rohypnol was by far my favourite and I would take four or five in a night, on the sly without telling anyone. I also wasn't averse to taking a load more K without anyone knowing. I remember going to the Cock Tavern, which had steep steps leading down to the basement. I blacked out going down them and fell forward. My friend Lisa caught me and carried me down the stairs.

The blacking out wasn't so much the issue, but everyone was shocked at how easily Lisa had carried me – I'm six foot one and she's five foot something and she carried me like a paper bag. From there it became farcical. They couldn't wake me up so someone emptied a bag of coke out over my top lip just under my nose, the reasoning being that every time I breathed in, a little bit would go up and that, eventually, I would breathe in enough to give me a buzz and boom, the show would go on . . . My friends Lisa and Stratty were going mental, but the party boys couldn't have given a fuck about my well-being. If I was unconscious, then the party wasn't happening.

The people I was surrounding myself with were getting worse and worse. Lisa and Stratty had been my clubbing mates for years and were the only ones still around, apart from Johnny and my friend Edna. Everyone else had left. There hadn't been an A-lister in my orbit for a long time.

To anyone who still had a foothold in normal society, I was way too much for them. We would have a laugh but I would always take it to the next level and I would fuck them off sooner or later. All they'd need to say was, 'I think you need to slow down,' and I'd say, 'Fuck you – you're gone,' and move on. George used to say to me that I was like a mafia boss. There were so many people around me and it was really hard to get an audience with me. So many people you had to go through to talk to me. Some friends had stood up to me so I just banned them from every club. As far as I was concerned, they were finished and dead to me. I would play people off against each other, and bully people to breaking point. I was vicious.

At the very, very end of the road, there was a couple I befriended – he was a DJ and wanted to break into the gay club scene and his wife looked like something out of *Bad Girls*. They were desperate for a way into the scene, I was desperate for drugs, and in order to pay for drugs, I needed to play. It helped that this so-called DJ would turn up every night with a bag of CDs after I said he might be able to play, and then I'd take them and play them as my own. At this stage I had lost all my music all over the place. I'd leave a bag of CDs at one chill-out, then another at another. I'd have to grab bunches of records from people and play whatever I could. This was way before you could turn up with your entire set on a memory stick.

At home, I had a room full of records, floor to ceiling. I just wasn't capable, or ever straight enough, to go there, sort them out and put a set into a record box and go clubbing. I had no clothes either, I would leave things everywhere. I would wander from one gig to the next via someone's house.

I'd borrow a top, or some jeans, leave my old ones there and go on, then I'd swap that again at someone else's. We would be in the DJ booth and would have to gaffer tape my jeans together. It was fucking skanky, but we were on this fucking rollercoaster and it seemed funny and ridiculous that we were having to stick my clothes together with tape.

I didn't care. When you're so lost in addiction, you don't care about any of those things in the way a normal person would. So long as I could wing it and get by, I was fine. I had one fucking tooth left, for Christ's sake, and I stank, but we would just keep going. The hedonists were looking for someone to normalise their behaviour. If I was acting worse than everyone else, then it made them all okay, and I was happy to play that role. Wherever we went, it always ended up being this messy, druggy, dirty scene. There could be ten of us in the toilets all just doing drugs or whatever, and I was the Pied Piper.

There used to be a twenty-four-hour gay cruising club in King's Cross. Upstairs was a bar where everyone would be allowed and downstairs was men only, which was where they'd have sex parties and people could cruise. We wouldn't be going for the sex, but it was always open and you could easily lose a day or two in there. It was the perfect hideout for someone like me – dark, sleazy and totally off grid. I remember Johnny turning up and screaming at all the bar staff whilst I was hiding in the back or in some maze downstairs: 'Why are you letting him in here? Can't you see the state of him? You're killing him and you're going to have his death on your hands.' By then I would have escaped out the door leaving them to deal with him and my mess.

We would hardly ever go back to mine. For a start, I wasn't capable of entertaining. It would be a bomb site and I'd never have any food or drink in the house. But if we did go back to mine I would be so far gone. Everyone would be downstairs playing silly off-your-head-type games, while I was sat upstairs, looking out of the window waiting for something to happen, and pranged-out-to-fuck paranoid and hallucinating.

I would do anything. Smoke anything – everything apart from heroin. I had morals about heroin because I looked down on smackheads. I revelled in the fact that I had a cocaine problem and I used to say to people when I had no teeth, 'Do you know how much money it takes to look like this?'

In those days, eating was a once-a-week activity. Somewhere around Tuesday or Wednesday, once we'd chilled out and I'd had a proper night's sleep and recovered slightly, I would go for pie and mash with Johnny or Lisa. But we would never ever eat mid-bender. Ever. I remember one time near the very end, I'd passed out and I'd started to come round. Normally, my first priority would be a JD and Coke and a line, but I was so weak that I needed food . . .

'Can someone get me a burger?' I said. 'What?!?' The whole room literally stopped, you may as well have turned the music off. 'Tony, it's only Sunday. Is everything all right?' 'I really need to eat,' I said, 'someone just get me a fucking burger.'

Everyone's faces said the same thing . . .

'Fuck. Tony is not okay.'

13.

I Thought You Was Dead

No one ever really believed I would go through with rehab. I think a lot of people thought it was a bit of a stunt. I remember seeing George before I went in – we weren't really speaking at that point and he was like, 'Yeah, right. Okay. Whatever.' That pretty much summed up everyone's attitude. I mean, that incident at The Cross was at the beginning of December and by Christmas Day I was wrapped up in a rug on the floor of my dealer's house like a giant sausage roll. It was understandable.

Johnny came with me to see the doctor. It was the first time I'd gone to see a professional and admitted there was something wrong and that I needed help. They put me in touch with a drugs drop-in centre on City Road. You had to show that you'd been making an effort to be clean in order to get into rehab on the NHS, and it took me three to four months from the moment of deciding I was going to give it a go, and finding someone to work with, to get to the stage of even being able to contemplate going cold turkey. They understood that you needed rehab to do that, but before they would give you a space, you had to turn up and report in for thirty days straight to show that you were at least trying to sort yourself out. I worked with a lady called Penny Chequer. I used to go in to see her every evening at these one-on-one classes she ran, along with a drug and relapse prevention programme. I remember her saying to me one weekend, 'Why don't you try not to do drugs this weekend?' Because they give you a drugs diary and you have to write in what, where and how many drugs you did. So, of course, what I did was lie. I didn't put in half of what I had taken. 'Oh, I only did two grams this whole weekend.' 'Oh Tony, that's lovely,' and I'm like, *Yeah, isn't it, good job you don't know about the rest.*

I was lying to them and to myself just so that I could get the praise. And everyone else in the group could go, 'Well done, Tony!' I'd be like, 'Yeah, I know!' Anyway, after I'd got to this fictional point of managing to cut down my drug use, Penny said to me one session, 'If you're going to go out this weekend, why don't you try to not take any drugs and just drink?' I'd never once thought that I had a drinking problem, so I said, 'Okay, yeah I will.' And I thought, *I'm going to do this.* Then I got so, so drunk. On the Friday I ended up in the police station in King's Cross for fighting. Then on the Saturday, I was so drunk I didn't go to work. I was so blasted, I was vomiting and unconscious in the flat. It was mayhem. Then, the following weekend, I did exactly the same. I remember throwing a pint glass at someone across the room and it smashing on them. I picked up a pool cue and whacked it over someone's head. It was chaos. That's when I realised, okay, we do have a drinking problem.

I mean, alcohol had never been a problem for me before because it was always counteracted by a shit ton of drugs.

I'd never got to the point where I'd been kicking off through booze. I'd always been able to have a few bumps to straighten myself out. Because I really looked down my nose at alcoholics, I thought they were total scum. Alcoholism was rife throughout my whole family and I thought they were the absolute worst of the worst. At least I had a class-A problem. At least I was hooked on the expensive drugs. Y'know?

Up until that point, I'd thought that if I could get help putting down the drugs then my drinking was fine. But it wasn't just drugs, it was alcohol – I was a fully fledged addict. When that realisation hit, rehab suddenly became very real. I realised that there was no going back, it was happening, and it was scary. Who was going to employ a DJ that didn't do drugs? How would I ever work again? What the fuck was I going to do afterwards?

I was still very much getting accustomed to the fact that I wouldn't use again if I went to rehab, and that I was going to have to be there for the next three, four or five months. I suddenly realised that it wasn't a matter of, 'Okay, this is going to be a holiday and then I can go back to my normal life and I've done what I said I would, and I've got help . . .' It was game over, it was giving up thirty years of my life, it was going to change everything and suddenly it was really daunting.

I caught the train there on my own. Johnny, Reggie and Tailor all came to Waterloo Station with me to say goodbye. Reggie and Tailor were our dogs – we got Reggie from my brother Kevin. He had this dog called Chico who was a nightmare and they weren't coping with him. We wanted a dog but we'd never got around to it and so we went to my brother's and met Reggie (nee Chico) and took him home there and then. A few years later we decided we wanted to get him a little pal and found Tailor. She was actually a guilt present toward the end of the relationship, but those dogs were my rock. I mean, I was a terrible dog owner but I made it up to them when I got sober. I remember crying the whole way there on the train – I knew this was what I wanted to do, but the tears were constant from the moment of setting off. Maybe it was the relief that it was actually happening, and fear because I didn't know what to expect. I kind of just thought, *Oh my God, this is the end of it. This is the end.* I wasn't crying because I was saying goodbye to drugs, they had totally lost their appeal by then, but I still struggled on a daily basis with my addiction. There had never been a moment where I'd thought, *This is my last line!* I was terrified of the change. I would always tell people that my life was shit, but it was my shit.

My rehab of choice was a place in Bournemouth called Allington House. The NHS is an amazing thing, and I'd been given the option to choose where I wanted to go from a selection offered. I quite liked the idea of being in Bournemouth because it had a big sandy beach and I thought, *Oh, I could hang out on the beach.* Suddenly I had gone from junkie to beach boy. I imagined myself playing volleyball on the beach like a freak, the one-toothed wonder who suddenly discovered a hidden skill for beach sports and was the absolute star. So I'd visited a few there and chosen Allington. When I first arrived there, I absolutely hated it. *Hated* it. I walked in and just shuddered. I suddenly realised that I was no longer in control of not being in control. I thought, *Okay, this is the end of the line. I either do this or I die.*

Everyone has a preconceived idea of what treatment is,

normally conceived from some bad ITV drama, or straight-to-TV film. Although the rules are essentially the same, rehab has evolved a lot since I was there, it's loosened up a fair bit and now isn't anywhere near as drastic as people assume. As an addict, to get yourself to rehab takes an awful lot of courage, but it's not the 'lock them up and throw away the key' scenario that people might assume.

There were blanket restrictions: for the first seven days you weren't allowed to use the phone, you weren't allowed out, and you weren't allowed music. You weren't allowed visits for the first four weeks and you were given a very strict settling-in period. That's all a lot more relaxed now. You would have to hand in your phone and then you would get it back at the end of your treatment. Now, when I'm sponsoring someone, one of the first things I tell them to do is to get rid of their smartphone and get a basic Nokia. Just think how much trouble you have access to with your smartphone . . . true, isn't it?

Often, when people first go into treatment, they feel so homesick and miss people back home, so the idea behind not allowing calls or visits is that, if family and friends came too soon, the client might just want to get into the car and go home with them. That first month is the most critical stage of treatment – also, for some patients, the physical side effects of detoxing can be quite severe, so sometimes it's kinder to the family not to see them.

Allington wasn't some big country house – I would have quite liked it if it had been. It was a modern detached house, nicely decorated but not a lavish hotel – remember all of my treatment was paid for by the NHS. You'd go in through the hallway where the phone was and through another door to the meeting room where you did all your group work. Then there was another group room, a few bedrooms on the ground floor, the counsellors' office, and upstairs were more bedrooms. It was a house. They were very much like student hall rooms – from what I knew of the ones I'd dossed at anyway – with simple single divan beds – you definitely weren't checking into fucking Claridge's. It had gardens around it where you could go and sit to have a bit of space, and there was a smoking shack at the bottom of the garden.

The first few days I did everything within my power to be thrown out. I mean, the first day I was really nice to everyone. Well, as nice as I knew how to be – I guess I was probably a little bit over the top and smarmy, to be honest. I walked in and sat on the side of a table in the living room. Havaiana flip flops and distressed baggy trousers were all the rage – it was 2007 – and I sat on the table with my legs hanging off, clacking the sole of my right flip flop up and down, *clack, clack, clack, clack, clack, clack*. It would get faster or slower, depending on my stress or anger levels. Anyway, I sat on the side of the table and Zoe, one of the counsellors walked in. I was clacking away and went in for the kill. 'Hiiiii baaaabe, so nice to meet you.' It didn't wash. 'Don't ever call me babe again and stop sitting on that table.' Christ, this was going to be a fun few months. I'd get her. And that was before I'd found out that I'd be sharing a room . . .

The rooming situation wasn't ideal. Essentially, all the new arrivals had to share and then you 'graduated' to having your own room. I was apoplectic. I couldn't fucking share – I was Fat Tony. The cheek of it. Eventually, I agreed that I would do it for one night and that they would have to find me my own room by the following day. I'd realised that my proposed roommate was quite hunky, so it suddenly didn't seem like quite such an imposition. He wanked non-stop by the way, seriously . . . I walked in on him so many times. But I was so grand, it was really quite unbelievable. I thought I was better than everyone else there – I was quite a piece of work. I really did think everyone was a basic fucking Bournemouth bitch, and I made sure that they knew it. As far as I was concerned, all Bournemouth had to offer was sunbeds, TK Maxx and cheap fillers.

I had told myself that there was no need to play the HIV card. I didn't need to, I was there for drug abuse and it never needed to be mentioned. But within three minutes I was like Dale Winton on fucking speed. The doctor wouldn't give me the inhalers that I wanted for my asthma, so I kicked up an almighty drama, shouting and screaming and saying things like, 'How dare you? You know I need them for my chest and my HIV.' My lungs were so fucked from taking drugs, I sounded like Darth Vader half the time. So I did play that card, straight away, but it wasn't just that, it was all very dramatic. There was so much complaining, nothing was ever, ever okay.

Every day at Allington was the same – they encourage routine to help with recovery. We'd have to be up for 7.30, tidy our rooms and then go down for breakfast. One of the jobs of house leader – which was a position I'd decided I wanted as soon as I'd become aware of it – was to knock on everyone's doors to wake them up. Somehow I got made head of house two times – but there was no knocking, I would run around kicking and banging everyone's doors and wake them up in the loudest way possible, and some of the guys there were pretty jangly at the best of times.

Breakfast was always Sugar Puffs. You don't need teeth to be able to eat those, do you? And then we were meant to go into the front room for 'Just for today', which is making a promise to yourself that you'll get through today and deal with tomorrow when it comes. We were then meant to meditate which, for me, never really happened. I would just sit there laughing and pulling faces.

One of the big rules in rehab is not to form any 'exclusive relationships', platonic or sexual. This is so no one feels excluded, to make sure everyone feels safe and that no cliques start to develop, which can turn into bullying. I completely ignored that rule and made friends with the tallest girl there: Collette. She was my first sober friend really; up until that point I'd wanted something from everyone I knew, normally drugs. I think she was the first person I just wanted as my friend. And we were awful: she actually really encouraged me to be a better version of myself, but by having her as my friend I had backup, and that, in my hands, was very dangerous because I felt like I had a little gang. Bully, me? No one would fucking dare call me a bully. I made sure of that, but I really was.

If anyone ever challenged me, they would be challenging Collette, too. We'd both gang up on everyone – if they even dared to pick a hole in my behaviour, Collette and I would come at them with all guns blazing. 'I'm not fucking having this, you're all fucking cunts, I'm packing my bags so fuck you.' They would get all this screamed right in their faces. People would be scared to come into the room if it was just me and Collette in there.

The 'List' was something that we would carefully construct each night in preparation for taking it with us to the

Concerns Group the following morning. Writing the list was my main pastime whilst at Allington. You were encouraged to speak up if you were concerned about someone else in the house, write out your concerns, explain them and try to use them to encourage and support them. Most people had one or two, but fuck that, my list was like a receipt roll and out it would come from my pocket each morning and I'd start laying into people. We weren't meant to go into each other's bedrooms but every evening Collette and I would get together and make up reasons to be concerned about someone in the group and then she could back my list up.

I'd start by saying something like, 'I'm concerned that Becky's going to drink today.' She'd go: 'Why?' 'Just the way you've been with me the last few days, and the way you've been acting up. Yesterday I said something to you and you were very confrontational.' It would all be bollocks, I would make up stuff and Colette would be like, 'Yes, I saw that too.' We'd sit there like the class bullies. We were awful. And Harry, my roommate, never got off lightly either . . . 'And my second concern is for Harry. I walked into the room yesterday and he was masturbating again.' Every day. I was such a cunt.

After that we would go into meditation, and then Peer Evaluation, which we renamed Peer Assassination. All your peers were given a sheet with a list of resources and blocks to recovery and they would have to tick a minimum of three and a maximum of six on each side and give a load of examples. You would do it for each other. 'How do you think Tony's behaviour was today?' 'How do you think Tony's recovery is going?' 'Do you think he's settled in well?'

Loads of stupid stuff like that. My sheets on everyone were always full on both sides. But if I had to answer anything on myself, you would have thought I was a saint.

I was the biggest hypocrite going. My defence mechanism was to keep everyone at arm's length. People were scared of me because I was brutal. You were meant to work on your self-esteem and anger management while there, but I did neither. Firstly, I didn't think I needed to do any work on my self-esteem and anger was my life force. I could talk the talk and I could raise my voice – and I would. I always had to be the loudest person in the room and had absolutely no problem with that.

One of the main exercises there was to write your life story and then read it out to the rest of the group. You know mine by now, but my life story as the rest of the group at rehab heard it? That was something quite different. You could have made like a fucking six-part movie out of it. There were car crashes, explosions, high-speed chases, I may as well have been jumping from a helicopter into a blazing inferno. When you tell your story, you want people to be impressed by your drug-taking and hear about how hard it was for you, so you might slightly embellish the truth. When most people tell their life stories, it's almost as though they want to convince you that they qualify to be in rehab. So they invent visits to the police station, stays in prison. You want people to think that you've been through absolute hell and that's the reason you're there.

I remember everyone crying as they listened to my story. I talked about losing boyfriends, the pain I was in and the destruction it caused. I never ever mentioned my hand in hurting others, of course, but I did talk about abuse. I wanted people to feel sorry for me. To think, *Oh, this is why Tony's the way he is,* because that's what you do throughout addiction, you look for justification. I used to tell people my dad died so that people would look at me and think, *Oh, that's why he's such a mess.* You play the pity card. Always. That's what addiction is about for people. It's a dangerous game where you make people feel sorry for you instead of taking responsibility for yourself.

The lowest point of my rehab stay came after sharing my life story. This Scottish guy there said that he wouldn't eat off the same plates as me because I was HIV positive. That was bloody awful. In fairness, I'd never got on with him anyway, there are so many different walks of life being brought together – he was in there for alcohol, and you know that I thought I was better than alcoholics – I was a London party boy who had lived in a bubble for the last thirty years. He told his friend that he wouldn't eat off the same plates or use the same cutlery as me because I had HIV, then the friend told me and I went and smashed all the plates on the floor and said that now he didn't need to . . . I brought it up in the next group session because it had actually really affected me. HIV and AIDS were such a part of everyday life on the gay scene in London. I wasn't used to such a personal attack. In the group he said he wished I would die of AIDS, and so they kicked him out. Typical – I'd spent all my time trying to get kicked out and someone else got thrown out instead.

Friday nights in rehab were a struggle for me. On a Friday the club night Fiction was still going, and I would have been playing there had I not been in Allington. So, every Friday I would pack my bag and pick an argument with one of the other clients or the carers and try my absolute hardest to get thrown out. At first the counsellors would pander to it and try and persuade me to stay, 'Come on Tony, you don't want to do that . . . why don't you go and have a cigarette in the garden and we can talk about it after that?' Then by about week three or four they'd sussed me out and were like, 'Go on then, see you . . .' I remember Easter was coming and that was a pretty low one because Easter had always been a big old four-day party weekend. Suddenly it was like, what the fuck, why am I not going to enjoy this like the rest of the world? I did everything in my power, apart from burn the place down, to get thrown out. I'd start arguments with everyone, say that I didn't want to be there, that I hated it. That the food was shit. I mean, it was quite 'mum' food, cottage pie, sausage and mash, stuff like that, but it wasn't awful. I was just a total monster. Screaming 'Look what the fuck you've made me do' as I packed may bags, or 'I'm going, fuck you all.' I could have left the house and walked to the bus stop and come back but it never even got to that. I'd tell them I'd stay another hour and think about it. My behaviour was what you might expect from a petulant teenager. I was so, so dramatic.

God knows where I thought I was going. I had nowhere to go, I couldn't leave. Plus, I wanted to get clean – I knew that was the only option left for me. My biggest kick-off was when I told them I had to go back to London to play Pride, my counsellors told me I couldn't do it. I argued that it was a community thing and made it into this huge problem that they weren't allowing me to be gay and be with my community. So we had to take it to group. In the end, I got my own way but I caused absolute hell. I went to

Pride – but had to be taken there by a counsellor and then brought back. During the first half of treatment, you have to have someone with you to go anywhere – I even had one come up to London with me when I got fillers. The early HIV drugs that I'd been on made my face really gaunt and burnt through the fat, making my cheeks and under my eyes really hollow. Add to that a drug problem, not eating and living on Coke and JD, and you're looking at a right mess.

One of the consequences of me saying they weren't allowing me to be gay was that I had to go to the local gay recovery group in town. It was fucking awful – there were about three people there – two old queens who were nearly dead, and some basic sexless lesbians. The joke was on me that time.

There would be moments when I just felt bleak. When new people were coming and going, the dynamics would change so much, and when you're there for six months, you see a lot of people come and go. Some would arrive and I'd be like, 'Oh God, what are these people like?' And there would be a weekly power struggle when they were dishing out the cleaning jobs. The worst job was cleaning the toilets. Fuck that. Twenty-odd people used those toilets every day and I wasn't cleaning up after them all.

Those who had been in the house the longest could apply to be house leaders, and everyone looked up to them. So, logically, after the first week of sussing it all out, I thought, *Right, as soon as they go, I'll take over.* That was my frame of mind, well, half the time. The rest of the time I was plotting to get myself sent back to London. Then at least I could say, 'Oh, I tried my best but it didn't work.' I'd blame it on the rehab instead of on me. If I got thrown out for being gay, which was my theory, then that would have been a win–win situation, but however much I pushed, I never got thrown out. Things felt very tough after being there for a month or so. The mask had started to slip – I was finding it harder to keep up the act and play the mega-cunt and things were starting to get real.

While in rehab you take the first three steps of a twelve-step programme. These first steps involved a lot of writing, you have to give examples of how you're powerless around addiction, and I would be having counselling alongside it. It was the first time I'd had one-to-one counselling and I remember quite liking it – of course I did. I was being given full air-time. I do remember the first time I met Zoe, my counsellor, and thinking that she looked like she belonged there, that maybe she'd spent a fair bit of time in rehab herself. She had this blonde bob, and was wearing bootcut jeans and this little suede jacket, and I thought she looked all right. Then I pissed her off by calling her babe and I was like 'Bring it on, bitch!'

For the first six weeks in rehab, I was doing what I needed to do to get off the drugs, but none of the background work on what had made me the person I was. I would like to say that there was a big turning point when a light suddenly went on, but it's really a gradual change, one foot in front of the other, and quite often it's only when you're graduating from rehab that you can see just how far you've come. It makes me emotional whenever I go back to rehab to give a talk or visit. It changed my life, it changed me, and whenever I visit, it makes me realise just how much I've changed. And I thank God I can go home again afterwards.

The second half of treatment is about starting to get you

ready to go back into normal life. Part of that is allowing you more freedom, so you're allowed out on your own. Even throughout the first half of treatment, the doors are never locked and there are bedrooms on the ground floor so there really is a lot of trust in there . . . I would do my chores and groups in the morning and then go out to the beach and the town for a few hours, and that was when I developed my obsession with sunbeds. I would go every single day, whack it up to the longest time and sizzle. I completely changed colour, bearing in mind I still had no teeth and was completely emaciated. Now I was tangerine-orange to boot.

I remember one day, I went out and had been doing my usual lap of the town – having a root through TK Maxx, going to the sunbed shop, my usuals. One of the counsellors was a massive Robbie Williams fan so I bought her a Robbie Williams stationary set . . . obviously, I made sure she thought it was a piss-take and ripped the shit out of her. But that's the thing about me – I like to make everyone think I'm a cunt, but I can be quite a sentimental old sod really.

When it's time for you to leave rehab, you have a graduation and get given a plaque, which is passed around everyone, and someone gives you away and makes a speech, and then you say something too. It's about giving you the best launch into the real world, really. I can't remember what I said but I'm sure I used it as an opportunity to decimate everyone around me.

You generally do three to six months in rehab. I did five and then they encourage you to stay in the area for another three months in supported housing. The theory is – and it's true – that when you step off the train back in London, or Leicester, or wherever you're from, there will be so many triggers that you'll relapse. Now, they make sure to create an aftercare package for you no matter where you stay, but they wanted me to move into shared housing in Bournemouth. Not on my fucking watch.

I was lucky that it worked out for me – there were still so many issues that I hadn't worked on. On the one hand, I was going back into a relationship that was absolute carnage, and on the other, I was going back into the club scene. I like to say that I was never scared of a relapse, but it was always there in the back of my mind, and there were still times that I would think, *Oooh, that could be a good idea.* The odds were stacked against me if I went back to London – everyone knew it. In my last one-to-one session with my Zoe, she told me I shouldn't go back to London, that I shouldn't go back to DJ'ing, that I shouldn't go back to my relationship. I explained to her that I wasn't going back to anything. I was going forward.

Life is always about moving onwards.

14.
The Pink Cloud

The Pink Cloud is a well-known phrase in recovery – it's when you first get clean, you come out and you think, *Oh God, I've cracked this. This is my new life.* Everything is amazing. AMAZING. You're back home and suddenly you start seeing everything around you as if you're seeing it for the very first time – you have these wisteria moments, as George and I called them. We were walking along in Hampstead and went past a wisteria tree in full bloom. I was like, 'Fuck, look at that tree. It's amazing.' George would be like, 'What?' And I'd be saying, 'No, look at that. It's incredible.' For all those years, you're so consumed by yourself that you don't see anything beyond it. You live for the night and you look at the floor – being out in the sun and looking up at the sky was something completely new to me. It was like discovering the world all over again.

When you leave treatment you think, *I've done it, I'm cured.* The first few days, or if you're lucky, the first few weeks after leaving, you think you are sorted. But very quickly you learn that you still have a long way to go. It wasn't that I craved drugs or alcohol – sometimes I would have moments when I would like something to change the way I was feeling – but you have to remember I'd really got to the end of the road with everything. I'd exhausted myself on them. You know, it's a process. I started going to meetings and I started to get better, because the thing you realise in treatment and afterwards is that the drink and the drugs weren't really the problem. I was.

I had to stop and sit down and work out a game plan of how I was going to keep getting the support I needed. I started one-on-one counselling and I went to meetings every single day because, remember, I had to find a whole new way of life. It wasn't about me coming back and being celebrated as 'Hurray, Tony's back!' Because I'd really fucked everything up, I had to work so, so hard to rebuild the bridges I had burned. I had really destroyed everything so I had to come back and be humble and try and repair some of the damage. It was really difficult, and especially for someone like me, who had such a huge fucking ego problem. I had to get real. It was the first time in my life where I thought, *Okay, you've got to do the work now*. Up until that point, I'd never really worked – of course I'd worked promoting clubs, DJ'ing and doing gigs. But I had never had to really work on having to rebuild my life because I'd always got by. But in the run-up to rehab, I had dismantled my life brick by brick, then I'd fucking sold the bricks for drugs.

My old life had gone. I was having to start afresh and work out what I really wanted. I wasn't sure if I wanted to go back to DJ'ing. I wasn't sure if I wanted to be in the relationship I was in. I was learning who I was again. I was rediscovering my sense of humour, but I was still acting up.

My head was telling me that I was still a cunt, and that my behaviours were funny and that I could get away with it. Because the one thing I had learned in treatment was that I was responsible for my behaviour, I was no longer blaming things on drink and drugs – I was no longer, 'Oh, it's Tony, he's funny,' or, 'Oh, he's a junkie, he's got a problem, this is what he does.' I didn't have anything to blame it on, I just had to admit that I was in recovery and it was going to take a long time to repair this stuff, and myself. That was just how it was.

I slowly started to reconnect with everybody from my past, the people I'd stopped seeing as addiction had taken over and as my world had got smaller and smaller. Old friends started to come back one by one. I think Davina McCall might have been the first. She was taking a meeting just outside of London and I remember seeing her and she was like, 'I thought that you were dead!' She asked me if I'd go with her and tell my story and I remember catching the train to Surrey, or somewhere like that, and going to this little place on the Monday. Telling my story for the first time after rehab felt so alien. To actually be honest and tell the truth about my life felt unnatural and very over-whelming. I felt so vulnerable afterwards, it wasn't like I felt this big wave of relief wash over me. It made me feel completely raw. Afterwards Davina was like, 'I'm so sorry, I had no idea, I really did think you were dead.' And that's how it was with people, that's what they thought. Because I'd been so hidden from people, I'd slipped further and further into such a little bubble where I hadn't seen daylight for years. I'd DJ'd and then would be holed up somewhere off my head and would only come back out at night for another DJ set, and the places I was DJ'ing were getting less and less glamorous and people just wouldn't have seen me.

The anxiety I had around going back to work was awful. How the hell was I ever going to go back to DJ'ing again? Who the hell would want a sober DJ? I'd never, ever once played a track sober, even in the early days, I'd been drunk. I just couldn't get my head around the idea of playing music completely straight. So I went to meetings and made recovery my priority. Because, although I had put down the drink and drugs, I hadn't dealt with the problem behind it. It's a bit like the house – you paint the hallway and then look at the front room and realise how shabby that looks. That's exactly how it is, it's a process, a very long-winded process. But it's also an amazing process when you do it properly.

I was desperate to move on to the next stage, though. Patience had never been my strong point. I wanted to listen to success stories, which is why I'd come back to London – I wanted to be a success story. I say to people now that they should use treatment as a springboard into their new life. That you treat the problem, and then you move on, you don't stay in the problem. You go to a treatment centre, you learn the new way to live and then you take those tools and you move forward. You can't stay wrapped in cotton wool forever.

On the train on the way home from rehab, I remember I was just so happy to be going home; my life had stood still for six months, and I wanted to move forward and I wanted to move on fast – that and order an Indian takeaway for dinner. Like I've said, my life was shit, but it was my shit. To come back to London and move forward with my life, and be excited about new beginnings, and how I was going to be in my relationship and work and be sober was a really big thing. It was exciting but it was also a lot to get my head around. It wasn't fireworks and Gay Pride marches, it was hard work every day. Hard to make relationships work that had only ever been based on drink and drugs. It was about putting one foot in front of the other, and those were very heavy shoes. All I'd ever been good at for twenty-eight years had been taking drugs and, to be honest, I hadn't been much good at that for the last ten years . . . But I was a survivor and I had defence skills, I was going to make it work.

Me being me, I got itchy feet within the first month and I wanted to start getting back to work, I wanted to be seen to be going out again, but on my terms, sober, and most importantly, the ego needed feeding. Badly. So what did I do? I placed my rehab diaries in *QX* and set about making a big return to London. *QX* was a slightly niche gay magazine that was given out free at every gay bar and club in town and was massive on the gay clubbing scene – my perfect market. So this was how I decided to announce my return. While I should have been solely focused on my recovery, I did all the interviews for *QX*, did a photoshoot, with me surrounded by muscle men in swim trunks. I'd had so much filler put in my face and I blew out my cheeks for the photoshoot so it looked like I had teeth and a jawline.

It wasn't long before the ego took over. 'Okay, I've arrived, everyone. I'm back!' I set up this big 'Fat Tony's first gig back' at the Raymond Revuebar. We took it over one Saturday night for my big comeback and it was just awful, it was like the worst New Year's Eve and birthday party rolled into one. People came with expectations of seeing me play and being different, and I don't think I could have done a worse job if I tried. I played one record, freaked out and said that I couldn't do it, and passed it to someone else. I couldn't even tell you what track I played.

It was all too much, too soon. It was only about two months after getting back to London and I wasn't ready. But I needed to work, I was living off sickness benefit but I knew that I could make money if I started playing. I wanted to stay clean and I knew I could be out in the club environment and make money. The transition was about making music my life again and not drugs.

There's a period after you come out of treatment when you're coming off the system, you're coming off sickness benefit, which you get placed on when you go to rehab, and you're turning your back on all the wheeling and dealing and underhand work you've been doing for years to actually go legit, and you're a bit like. . . what? Rent? What the fuck is that? Learning to be responsible comes at a massive cost, and it takes time. That transition period took me a good couple of years, to be 100% honest. There's still a part of me that doesn't want to pay for cheese in Sainsbury's and there's still a part of me that doesn't really want to pay tax. I thought I was above having to deal with that shit.

In rehab, I had thought to myself over and over again that I was going forward to London, not back, and I was going to smash it. I was going to show everyone that I could do this clean and sober. It was really a case of sticking two fingers up at everyone who had said I couldn't do it. I'd thought about who was still in my circle – there were a lot of people who I couldn't have in my life anymore. But I never had to choose, really. They were like rats off a sinking ship . . . *vroom*, they saw me going down and they were gone. Part of me would like to say that it was about me coming back and proving to myself that I could do it and that it wasn't for anyone else, but that's bullshit. I wanted to show them all: 'Tony's back and he's still managing to do what he's always done but he's doing it sober!'

At six months clean, I thought I knew everything there was to know about recovery – even six hours clean was magical! To be six months clean, I thought I'd nailed it – no one could tell me anything. Most people are the same when they come out of treatment, but all they've really done is put down drink and drugs while they've been in a very safe and sterile place. They've been locked in a house for six months – of course they've not fucking done drugs, unless they've been sniffing the kitchen cleaner. The hard work starts when you come out.

It isn't a piece of piss. The therapy I started was intense, and it went on for two years after treatment. I went to this place in St James's, which was on the NHS as well, and if it wasn't for them I think I would be dead. They did an incredible job, they were all ex-junkies and everyone that worked with me and helped me had dealt with the disease. I think that's where the magic came from. It's the same as being a bereavement counsellor; you can't sit and help a woman who's lost her child and tell her truthfully that you know what she's going through unless you really have. It's the same with drugs – you can't tell someone unless you understand the life skills it takes to be a junkie. Don't you dare walk past someone on the street and judge them – you have no idea what's happened in their life to lead them to that place. How much effort it takes for someone to sit on the street every day and ask you for change. To re-enter a world you've only known through a drink and drug haze is terrifying. For me, I think that's why my ego took over. Egos come from a place of fear and, of course, I was scared shitless that I wouldn't be relevant anymore.

After sorting my treatment programme outside of rehab, the second thing to sort was my teeth. Even though I was so full of bravado, and had this ego that was carrying me along, it took me a lot of courage to go to a dentist and say, 'Look, this is what I've done to myself, what can we do to fix it?' I went, petrified and full of shame, and he was straightforward, and just said, 'Okay, I suggest we take everything out.' Because there were still broken stubs and broken bits of tooth in the gums. I mean, I hadn't really drunk water for about twenty-eight fucking years and had lived off a diet of Jack Daniels, Coca-Cola and drugs, so it was little wonder that I'd got into that state. In a way, this was about getting the strength and courage to say, 'This is who I am now,' and valuing myself enough to get them fixed. That might sound pretty straightforward to most normal people, but to an ex-junkie it's mind-blowing. Before, walking around in that state, with no teeth, I hid behind the fact that I was a drug addict. Now that I was back in the real world, I wanted to be respected, and I was learning self-respect. For me, taking that first step and going to the dentist and saying, 'Right, I need to sort my teeth,' took so much courage. I remember going there and sitting in the waiting room and sweating and thinking, *Oh my God, this is awful, they're going to judge me and think I'm scum.*

I was still in constant pain with my teeth, but had somehow

just got used to it and learned to live with it. I didn't take painkillers because I used to take Nurofen and codeine by the bucketload when my teeth were bad. I knew I needed to have all the teeth taken out, and then give them time to heal properly for them to be able to put new ones in. I was just gums for about three months, I remember calling my sponsor, Del, after they'd started taking them out and him being like 'Babe, I can't understand a word you're saying.'

Del was my first sponsor and was amazing. For the uninitiated, a sponsor is the person who guides you and listens to you and points you in the right direction on a twelve-step programme. They're someone who has worked the twelve steps and lives by them. They're like a guardian angel when you're working a programme. I still have so much love and care from Del even to this day. He likes to say that he went into five years of insanity with me when I came out of treatment, which I suppose he did. He also likes to say I only chose him as my sponsor because he wore head-to-toe Westwood to meetings and, again, he might have a point. Del was brilliant when it came to helping me sort my teeth. It would have taken eighteen months for the entire process on the NHS, and I'm not knocking them because they have done so, so much for me, but the idea of just having gums for that long was really quite depressing. He took me to his dentist in Oxford who said that he could start sorting my mouth out, and it was only at this point I could start to see the light at the end of the tunnel. I hadn't realised how much still not having any teeth affected me, but I could start to move forward. When they finally put them in, there was no stopping me. It was like 'Whoosh! Yes, she's arrived!'

Coming out of treatment, my social circle was quite small. There was Johnny, of course, and Bruce, who I'd known since Trade days. He'd been one of my trusty drug partners. Him, Stratty and Lisa were my gang and everyone else was just an entourage around us. Bruce got clean and we started going to meetings together. When I first started bumping into people again they were really awkward around me, no one knew how to approach me. George was the biggest one – I must have been out of treatment for about four months, and was crossing City Road with Johnny when he spotted George through his car window. He got out of the car off his nut and was so twitchy that his feet were doing the two-step. He couldn't hold the same position or stand still, he was so wired, and he tried to tell me he was clean. I remember him getting back into the car and me laughing with Johnny – I mean, bless him. He'd been my lifelong friend but he just didn't know what to do with me, and that's when I thought, *Right. I'm going to get that bitch clean.* I called him every day. Most of the time he wouldn't pick up but I didn't give up on him and he's now thirteen years clean. There were other complications, too. I couldn't walk down Broadwick Street or Berwick Street Market in Soho because I owed all the dealers money. There were other people I owed money to and I paid them back, but I never paid a drug dealer back – my theory was that once you got clean and went to rehab, all the money that you owed for drugs was wiped off the slate and somehow I got away with that theory. I mean, they weren't very happy about it but they couldn't argue that I hadn't done the time.

The thing about addiction, which I was quickly learning, is that it doesn't go away, it moves around. I can get into sewing, into cooking, into the gym or into shopping and unchecked, they can become addictive in their own right. Because you no longer have drink or drugs to alter your mood, I didn't have anything to change the way I was feeling, and there were loads of times when I had to take a minute and just think – this might not work, this might not be okay, I'm not sure I can cope with this, I don't think I can be sober. Dealing with myself and not having anything to alter my mood was sometimes just so, so hard. But I knew that the only option other than sobriety was death, and I really wanted to live. I knew I had to be sober and that if I failed, that would be it, but it was really hard dealing with all the other stuff. Life on life's terms, when you've always had buffers there, is hard. So you find yourself finding alternatives to drugs . . .

When I broke up with Johnny, I learned this more than ever. I never used, but I lost the plot. He'd caught me cheating and couldn't deal with it anymore. I was sober but I was lying and still doing many of the things I had done beforehand, this time without the excuse of drink and drugs. I think this must have gone on for two or three years and after everything we'd been through together, I was lost in an addiction yet again. I'd put down the drink and the drugs but the mindset was still there and I wasn't doing any work on myself. I was picking up other addictions instead, and he just couldn't take anymore.

After breaking up came my gym phase. I got this personal trainer who was this big Muscle Mary and joined the gay gym in Covent Garden – obviously – and started going every day. Then I went onto steroids for a while because it's all or nothing with me. I was really fit for about a year, then

I met this boy Jack and decided to take a week off to focus on him – because clearly, he was the one and I was going to marry him – and I never went back. I only started training again recently – although this time it's a healthy two or three times a week.

Then there was the stage when I really got into Botox and fillers. I mean, I lost it. My friend Ezra was a nurse who had set up a sideline in aesthetics and I'd go every week and pester him to put more in. I started to have my lips done, and then my cheeks done, and I'd be DJ'ing at these gay parties like Room Service or We Party with massive lips and ridiculous cheeks. When I drank a can of Coca-Cola it would spill out of the side of my mouth, and when I spoke to people I would be dribbling.

Then there was the time I got addicted to tanning injections. I was at Malcolm McLaren's funeral and Jeremy Healey put his hand on my shoulder and was like, 'Marnoch, you've changed colour,' and the late David Tang was saying I looked like George Hamilton. I was ridiculous. I was still dating Jack and was living at George's at the time; he wouldn't allow me to have boys over – well, not when he was there. Of course, when he was away, it was like the YMCA. Anyway, Ezra gave me the keys to his flat so that we could stay there. Jack and I had been out to Shoreditch House and then we went back to Ezra's and one of the side effects of the tanning injections was that it gave you an extended hard-on. It was to be our first night together and I wanted to make sure I performed so I popped a few Viagra as well, for good measure. We had sex and fell asleep, but I woke up an hour later and my penis was still erect and it was throbbing. I was trying to make it go down and it just wouldn't, so two and a half hours later, with it still throbbing, I was crying with pain. I called my doctor Naz, who was in LA at the time, and asked him what I should do. I mean, it was my fucking dick, anything else I'd have waited until the next morning, but seriously man, it was starting to change colour and go black. I was like, 'Naz, I've got a problem.' I explained what had happened, he said, 'You need to call an ambulance, you need to call an ambulance straight away.' Apparently, the blood could congeal in the penis and I would never get hard ever again. FUCK!

So I called 999, and spoke to the woman, whispering because Jack was asleep in the other room. I explained to her, 'I've got a problem. I've had an erection for eight hours . . .' 'Sir,' she said, and I was like, 'I'm serious, this is a serious phone call, I spoke to my doctor and he said I needed to call an ambulance.' So she said to me, 'What colour is your penis?' and I said, 'It's black and I'm white.' So she's like, 'Okay, let me speak to someone.' They sent a man out on a bike to me, and I was terrified Jack would wake up. Anyway, the ambulance guy turned up and was like, 'Let me take a look.' He took a cannula out, stuck it into the base of my penis and drained the blood. Jack woke up about an hour later, completely oblivious.

You see, there's another saying in recovery: if you take the rum out of the fruitcake what are you left with? Fruitcake. Fucking mental fruitcake.

15.

At Her Majesty's Pleasure

Twelve months out of rehab and a year into recovery, I was flying high on life. I remember someone saying to me in the dark days pre-rehab, 'If you could just put drugs down for a minute and take a line of yourself, you'd realise that's better than any high.' At the time I was like 'Oh, fuck off.' But they were right. I was going to twelve-step meetings every day, I was doing a lot of therapy, and work was building up – I was back doing clubs like Trade and the Egg.

Things at home with Johnny weren't perfect. We were back on our relationship rollercoaster and he was trying sobriety too – he was a few months behind me but he had made the effort of getting clean and we were both trying. It was a massive learning curve for both of us. Coming out of rehab and having sober sex was like being a teenager again, because those years had been stolen from me when I was a kid. We had hit a rhythm, we were working on it, and we were still together, at least.

I remember having lunch with my sponsor at the time, and him saying, 'You seem really happy and your recovery is going really well, but I'd love to see what happens when something really bad happens to you,' and I just remember thinking, *I'll be fine, thank you*. Nothing was fucking sinking this ship.

And then it happened: the lowest point of my life. Lower than rehab, lower than any of the situations I'd ended up in off my nut, lower than nearly dying of HIV. I was falsely accused of abusing an underage boy and sent to Pentonville Prison. I debated if I wanted to drag it all up again for this book . . . You see, after what I'd gone through, being abused as a kid, to be accused of doing that to someone else was the worst thing imaginable. It really affected me. But it's a part of my story, and there are no skeletons in my closet, so here you go:

It was almost exactly a year to the day since I'd come out of treatment and I was out walking Tailor, my dog, in Angel, North London. She was heavily pregnant at the time and this gang of teenage lads stormed past and knocked her. Now you don't do that to any dog, let alone my Tailor. I went fucking mental and threatened to smash their faces in, break their legs, the lot, and told them not to come near this area again. The next day, Johnny and I were going to see a film at the cinema complex in Angel when I suddenly found myself being thrown to the floor and pinned down by six police officers and arrested on the spot. No conversation, no warning, excessive force and boom, straight into custody. I remember being in the police cell and they wouldn't tell me what I was being charged with. All they would tell me was, 'You're being arrested for an inquiry.' I kept asking what for, and they wouldn't say.

I was kept like that in the cell, then this police officer came up to me, spat at me and said, 'You vile creature.' He asked me where I was the day before and I told him that I was visiting my friend Amy in rehab. They were like, 'Have you got proof of that?' I thought they had just got the wrong person and were going to let me go in an hour. He then said they were charging me with the rape of a fourteen-year-old boy and I was like, 'What the fuck!?' They asked if I wanted a lawyer and I was like, *Why the fuck would I want one? I haven't done anything wrong.* So I was interviewed without a lawyer and told them that I was a gay man and that I was abused as a child. They thought that made me an abuser – he's gay, he was abused as a child, and he's admitted to having one-night stands and promiscuous sex, therefore he must be a predator. Bingo! They thought they'd got their guy.

The ironic thing is that I had been to Pentonville Prison a month before. I was asked to give a talk to prisoners about recovery at an NA meeting. So, there I'd been on the C wing as these boys were running up and down the stairs in their grey tracksuit bottoms, and I'd thought to myself, *I could have some of this.* I remember thinking, *Oh, I'd love to be in here.* I did the meeting and left and then a month later I was in there. Be careful what you wish for.

Because I was a gay man and I had worked so much on myself, it really shook me that they could somehow pigeon-hole me and say that I had done this. But it was also perhaps the biggest turning point of my life. All through addiction, all through treatment, I'd still always had my ego, and I'd fed my ego and it drove me and gave me protection. Being arrested and accused of that completely stripped me. I was broken. Every day I would go from wanting to prove my innocence to wanting to kill myself. I knew I was innocent but they had thrown me in there and were treating me as though it was a done deal. I would think about ways of hanging myself in my cell because, how would I ever come back from this? The only thing that kept me going was the fact that I knew I was innocent. I was made to stand in court listening to people reading out what I'd been accused of, thinking, *What the fuck, there's absolutely no proof.* I was a fucking mess but Johnny, Scratty, Lisa, Kiera, all of my friends, everyone stood by me. They all believed in me, but it was fucking awful.

Whenever I tell people this story their first question is, 'Didn't it make you want to use?' But I never wanted to. Not once. You have to remember, I had been to such a dark, dark place using. You have to understand that I had absolutely kicked the arse out of coke. I had beaten it to death, and in turn, it had nearly beaten me to death. Every day there was still my addiction to struggle with but luckily I'd done enough work at that stage to know that if I used again then a) it was going to make me look like I had done something wrong and b) it wasn't going to make things any better. I was clean and I was looking after myself and I was responsible and I needed to show and prove that.

There were still God-given moments, throughout all of this. I'd been in police custody for four days before they transferred me to Pentonville. They'd questioned me and questioned me, over and over again, and there was a lot of psychological bullying at play. When I got to Pentonville this massive guy came into my cell and asked if I wanted any pills or powders. Then I said the magic four words: 'No, I'm in recovery.' 'Seriously?' he said, then he was like, 'You might know my girlfriend, she is too.' I mean, that's a bit like going on holiday to Magaluf and saying you're from London and someone saying you might know so and so . . . Or telling someone you're gay, and they're a bit like, 'Oh, you might know my Uncle Phil.' But I asked her name and he told me, and it turned out I'd been in rehab with her and I'd given her money to go and collect their kids from his mum's, and he remembered. 'You're that Tony! Anything you need in here, you tell me . . .' And within half an hour he had come back with a mobile phone and I could call my mum and Johnny, which was the boost I really needed.

I learned from my lawyer that the boy who had accused me had been abused and had been in and out of care. He accused me because I'd called him a fat cunt in Angel that day and threatened to smash his and his mates' faces in after they shoved Tailor. But, as far as the police were concerned, there's no smoke without fire, and in the UK we tend to accuse first, and ask questions later.

I spent six weeks in prison because I was on remand and the trial was pending. They wanted to put me in a special wing – the wing where they put prisoners who could be at risk from the other inmates, or a risk to themselves – and I said 'Fuck no, I'm not going there, I haven't done anything wrong'. I had to pretend I was in there for drugs because it was the most horrible thing ever. It was really harrowing. I kept thinking, *It's going to be on the news, there'll be no coming back from this, people will just believe the headlines.*

I think the most upsetting moment was me needing my HIV medication and having to sort it out in prison. I thought they would just get it from the prison doctor, but they took me to Chelsea and Westminster Hospital in shackles, not just cuffed, but chained to a police officer on each side.

They parked at the end of Fulham Road and walked me all the way down like that and then made me sit in the waiting room being stared at by everybody. My friend's boyfriend was working on reception, and even though there were whispers around the scene that I'd been arrested, no one knew anything. 'What the fuck happened, Tony?' I remember him asking me, and I was just like, 'Please can you get us into a private waiting room, I really don't want to be out here like this.' He did, and within minutes my doctor, Marta, came in and demanded they uncuff me. They said they couldn't but she was someone you didn't mess with, I remember her shouting at them, 'Give the man some dignity, uncuff him and wait by the door.' She asked me what was going on, and when I told her she just kept shaking her head. 'No, Tony, this isn't you. I know you didn't do this.' Bear in mind that she'd been treating me for a few years at that point. She was amazing, she wrote a letter to the judge and really threw her all behind getting me out, and most importantly she was the first person I'd seen face to face since the arrest who knew me, and that really gave me hope.

Johnny and Del set about getting me out on bail. They went to see my lawyer and he said that they were going to need at least £40k in cash to get me out. I had been back working for all the big clubs, and so off they went around London visiting everyone we knew and within three hours they had got the money. Laurence Malice from Egg put a load in, my old drug dealer put £10k in, another big club owner put in £5k – so many people helped get that bail money together. They all knew I was a lot of things but they knew I would never have done this. I got bail and was allowed out under house arrest and it was decided I would

With Danny Rampling   DJing at George Michael 30th Birthday

Being a monster with Leah   Photo by Brad Branson

trade it's hotter than a dog with two dicks – FAT TONY DJ

Tiger print hair-do

The two George's re-unite

Happy & Clean!

Portrait by TradeMark

Quick snog with Davina

Lily Allen & Lady Gaga

'Edna' Mark McKenzie

Lisa Allen

Del Murray (my first spon

With the lovely Kylie

With Blondey Gary Aspden (my sponsor)
Robert Broo

Photo by Boy George

I love my job!

At Kate's in the Cotswolds for Christmas

My Birthday with Kate & Naomi

Lucky Bitches with Joan Collins

With Paris Hilton & Kate

SHOWstudio
9-10-11 JULY
FASHION
DJS
87.7FM

with Kate Moss, Kelly Osbourne
Sam McKnight, The Pet Shop B
and Boy George

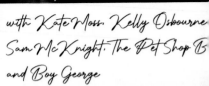

With David Furnish

With Jean-Paul Gaultier

With Victoria Beckham

With Kate & Naomi for Amfar

With Edward Enninful, Kim Jones & Dylan Jones

With the lovely Donatella Versace

Jodie Harsh, Elton John & David Furnish

'Fat / Moss' on the decks

My mate for decades Goldie

'No More Drama' with Mary J Blige

Tony's Angels -Bananarama

With David Beckham

My baby girl Tailor

years of friendship *Nile Rogers*

With my lovely Mum at my 50th Birthday

Norman Jay OBE

With Cher in São Paulo for Amfar

British Vogue Bafta party with date *Courtney Love*

With Luke Evans, Kylie Minogue, Jodie Harsh Kelly Osbourne & Jimmy Q

Recovery is Everything!

go and stay with my parents in Dungeness, and so, at the age of forty-two, I was back with Mum and Dad again.

By the time the court case started, it was coming up to the second anniversary of me being clean. It had been approved for me to stay at Boy George's house during the trial as I wasn't allowed to go back to mine in Islington. Of course, someone leaked the story and it ended up in all of the papers. 'Boy George Harbours Paedo DJ' read one head-line and it made it a hundred times worse for me; I got spat on in the street and threatened. People read that stuff and they believe the garbage, but I just thought, *Fuck you all, I haven't done a fucking thing wrong.*

On the first day of the trial, they read out all of these things you're accused of and it really is fucking awful. I'd had some low points in my life but that was the absolute lowest. I was sitting in the corner thinking, *I'm going to prison.* However awful it was, the court was full of my family and friends, who were there to support me. Not one person from the boy's family came to the trial. If that was my son, I'd be there every day, I would be after blood, but not one person was there.

My mum was there every day and you couldn't have got more people into the court if you had tried. The first day that I was in court the woman behind this glass box with me gave me the dirtiest look as they read out the charges. I remember asking her for a glass of water and she ignored me. They treated me like shit. They swore in the jury and there were three very straight-laced-looking middle-class women and I just thought, *They're not going to want to hear a gay man's story. I'm going down no matter what.* I remember leaving that day crying and saying to my mum, 'I'm going to prison. That jury isn't going to want to hear what I have to say, evidence or no evidence.'

The next day I got a phone call saying that a woman on the jury had suffered a miscarriage and that they would either have to replace her or the whole jury. Either way, we'd need to start all over. It was my choice and I chose to replace the whole jury. Hearing the charges once made me think I was going to prison; having the same jury listen to them twice wasn't going to help me. I changed the jury and this time it included what looked like three gay men. By the second day, the woman behind the glass caught me and said, 'Can I say something to you? I know you never did this.' I thanked her so much for saying that and she responded saying, 'I hear cases every day and I know when someone is guilty and I know that you are not guilty.' I said, 'Let's hope the jury does too.'

When all the evidence came back, my DNA wasn't found. Other men's was, but there was no trace of mine anywhere. I had been accused of holding a door shut with my hand, but my prints weren't on that door. The accuser said that I held him hostage, along with other melodramatic stuff, but none of it stacked up.

The police had said that the CCTV they'd obtained from the Angel multiplex was unusable but that it showed me going into a cinema on Saturday and put me at the scene of the crime. My lawyer's girlfriend used to work at the cinema and managed to get other CCTV, which showed there were people going in and out of the toilet I was meant to have been holding the boy captive in.

I was cleared of all charges, and the jury found me not guilty in under five minutes.

But you know what, even after all of that, the lowest of the low, I still believe that everything happens for a reason.

The time I spent with my parents during the trial was a gift from God.

I got to know my father in a way I never had before.

16.

Like Father, Like Son

My dad was a big old bloke. He was from an age when men were men, and he didn't have a feminine side at all. It wasn't that he hid one, there just wasn't one gene of femininity in his DNA. He was six foot one with fingers like bananas, and he really did put the fear of God into us. For good reason. My dad was a man who knew right from wrong, he had very strong morals – they might not have been the same morals as everyone else, but they were morals all the same. He was very staunch on what was wrong and what was right, if we got into a fight or someone punched us he'd throw us out of the house and tell us to go round and beat them up. 'You fucking go and sort them out or I'll sort you out.' Yes, my dad was a man of great dignity and he was strong as an ox.

He was the son of a sergeant major in the Scots Guards. He came from a family of incredible discipline. I can remember my nan, my dad's mum. She was a small woman with glasses like Dame Edna Everage – 1950s cat-eye shaped – but without the diamanté. She looked like she should be on the packet of Aunt Bessie's roast potatoes. She was so strict with us, there was no running around the house. 'Sit down!' would echo around the house on a Sunday afternoon when she was at ours. There was no messing around, and she would always leave at six on the dot. Even to this day, I can see her when I close my eyes. I remember my dad's brothers and sisters too, the whole family were incredibly strong characters. The ones that are still here still are.

My dad had three absolute tearaway sons, my older brother Kevin who, as I've already said, was always in trouble, and while I like to point the finger at him, I wasn't much better. None of us were angels, including my younger brother Dean. You know, we grew up on a council estate and hung around in gangs. It wasn't like it is now, but we were working-class kids and we were fucking scrappy, it wasn't like we were growing up in the countryside riding ponies. Even when I was really young I would be grounded because of something I'd done. I wouldn't be allowed to go out and would have to stay in my room, but that was better than my dad getting the belt out. I'd been a problem child from the age of about three onwards. I'd stab the new sofa with a kitchen knife, try to set fire to the house with matches, break shop windows – whatever there was to do, I would do it. Nowadays I would be diagnosed with ADHD or something like that, but back then I was just a delinquent. Add to that being the middle sibling and growing up gay and you've got a proper handful. As kids we'd hang around street corners in gangs. Back then it wasn't like we were going out stabbing or shooting people, but we'd get into as much mischief as we could. There were so many times the police would come to our house and it would be because I'd thrown a brick through a window or something like that. Not just because of Kevin.

I still remember the smell of my dad, and it's that sweet, musty smell of cigars. Even now when I smell cigar smoke it makes me think of manliness and strength. He was a sharp dresser too, my dad. Saturday night and the gold rings would go on with pressed Farah slacks, a shirt a little open and an alpaca fur coat. As a father, my dad was never the type to wear his heart on his sleeve. He never made any grand gestures of love, as in, 'You're my son, come here for a kiss and a cuddle.' I knew that he loved me as a very young child but not so much when I got older. There were still tender moments, Sunday mornings with Elvis on in the background stand out, but there came a stage when I latched on to preferring to remember him in a different way. When Dean came along, it changed everything. I felt like he was the golden boy and the son my dad really wanted. I'd been the son he'd had to put up with, dressing up in drag and running around the estate with a pair of plastic stuck-on tits, causing havoc. Then along came Dean, who was into everything little boys were meant to be into. You've got to give my dad credit because it was a different time back then and he didn't try and stop me being so camp or punish me for it.

My mum always says that I caused the most heartache. I remember when I was three and had a collapsed lung, my dad came to see me a lot in the hospital and every night I'd be like, 'Can I come home now?' And my dad would tell me that he and my mum were just going to ask one of the nurses and then they'd be back. They never came back. Well, not until the next day, but I remember I'd be waiting and waiting until I realised they'd done it again – and not to be melodramatic, but I think that always stayed with me.

Like most of us, my dad had his demons. When he drank,

he would turn, like people with a chemical imbalance do, and it didn't do him justice. He would only ever drink at the weekends, and it was when he would drink something like Scotch that he would become violent. He would be fine on beer and could drink that until the cows came home, but give him a Scotch and he would turn nasty. Us kids would hide in our rooms petrified and my mum felt his wrath on more than a few occasions. That's what I remember of my dad growing up. I held it against him for most of his life, and that made it really easy for me to blame him for everything.

I never needed to come out to my parents, they always knew. It was never something that was discussed. My parents never sat me down and made me talk to them about it. I think Patrick was probably the first person I took into my house and introduced as a boyfriend, and that wasn't until my mid-twenties. My little brother lived at home too, so I would normally just go off to other people's places, and you know, I grew up on a council estate in Battersea. It wasn't like you invited boys around for tea, there was no such fucking thing! The last thing my dad wanted was some boyfriend turning up – it was hard enough for him to contend with me flouncing around in drag without me bringing some boy home.

Gina would come around to the house all the time and Steve Strange would come over too, but there was never really talk of sexuality. In all honesty, I don't think they really cared that they had a gay son. I used to think that my dad didn't talk about it because he didn't approve, that he was homophobic and had an issue with it, but I was wrong – he actually loved me and everything I did. My mum used to tell me how proud he was of me and I'd argue with her that he wasn't. He just never wore his heart on

his sleeve and in retrospect it was probably my own inter-
nalised homophobia which made it an issue. I projected
onto him and decided he was a homophobe, and that
couldn't have been further from the truth, but it all added
to my version of him that I chose to believe.

When the big catastrophes like HIV and AIDS happened,
which are a big enough worry for a parent now, let alone
when they first came about, I never had a safe-sex chat
with him or my mum. Even Gina was drinking cups of tea
when we were around my parents, for fuck's sake – we
tried our best to pretend butter wouldn't melt. But my dad
was a teenager at the beginning of the swinging 60s. He
had been a seventeen, eighteen, nineteen-year-old at a time
of massive social change so I'm pretty sure he'd done his
own fair share of gear, to be honest. He used to go to clubs
and out partying every night of the week. That's how he
and my mum met. They would go to the Gate Club on
King's Road, which was a lesbian bar, so it's not as though
he had lived a completely sheltered existence.

He was very astute, my dad. When my brothers were
dabbling he would work it out before anyone else and go
and find whichever one it was and drag him out of the pub
and give them a slap. My dad was a very proud person in
that respect and, like I said, had a strong sense of right and
wrong. I think he knew what I was doing when it came to
drugs but also knew that he couldn't stop me. There would
be times I would come home absolutely off my tiny little
rocker and he would just look at me. He wouldn't even
need to say anything – that look would absolutely say it
all. It was a look of complete disappointment. The times he
did say something it would just be, 'Get yourself to bed.'

Even then I'd have to backchat – 'Why do you hate me so much?!' or something similar, would normally be shouted down the stairs before I slammed the door in defiance.

Even when I was hospitalised and nearly died, I don't think I ever had the HIV chat with my dad. He obviously found a way to deal with it because he never shunned me. I talk a lot about how my mum supported me through that, but whenever I refer to her helping me, my dad was always involved. I was a mummy's boy, but all of her actions were sanctioned by my dad.

It was after being hospitalised and diagnosed that my dad and I had our biggest falling out. The house my parents had given me to live in rent-free in Battersea when they had moved, our family home of over thirty years, had basically been turned into a crack den. I'd moved a ketamine dealer into one bedroom and a coke dealer into the other. The behaviour was out of control. I'd been having chill-out parties after we'd been clubbing from Monday mornings right through to Wednesday. We'd be playing music non-stop and it was like a fucking beach outside our house, all the gays lying out in the sun. The neighbours were all complaining, and because it had been a family home which all of a sudden the son had turned into a gay crack den, they were complaining to my parents.

I never knew what my dad thought of it because I stayed away from him after that, but I don't think he was very proud of me. I think he was at the stage of waiting to see just what I could do next. I had taken it to every extreme. It wasn't as though I'd run the house completely into the ground. It was still my home, there were still days of clarity where I would tidy everything up, there were just a lot of lost days and weeks. Johnny had moved in for a few weeks, but then he'd left because he just couldn't deal with it. Anyway, my family had had enough and decided to sell the house. I'd come out of hospital about six months earlier and was on the road to recovery, and they were there clearing out the loft and thirty years of family life, and I had to move.

My dad took his telly back off me. I was outraged – how could he? In his eyes, he was taking it back so I didn't sell it for drugs, but in my eyes, he was taking it back because he hated me. As you might expect, I kicked up an almighty fuss. I remember screaming, 'How can you do this to me? Do you know what I'm going through? Do you know how ill I am?' Always the victim. But I remember him turning around and saying, 'I'm doing this because you deserve this to be done to you.'

I was horrified. My father was saying that I deserved HIV because I was gay. That was my takeaway from that statement, nothing to do with the TV, and I didn't speak to him for three years. That wasn't what he was saying – he was taking the TV and selling the house because I didn't deserve it, I didn't deserve to be pandered to, and pampered and buffered from the reality of life. He thought I deserved it because I was causing havoc, breaking my mum's heart and taking a fucking ton of drugs. But for me, it was the ultimate free pass, I could go straight to blaming him for my actions.

My paranoid, delusional mind told me that he thought I deserved to be dying and that was absolute bullshit. They had given me a house rent-free and I had put them through absolute hell, and continued to put them through hell. I'd nearly died and still continued to be that person. Most people who are given a second chance, take that second chance with both hands. But I was a fucking addict and I was powerless to take it. Of course, I was going to go back to what I knew best. I didn't even relate the two things together – drugs and the fact that I'd nearly died. Of course, they were disappointed.

Even when I came out of rehab, I was still far too busy with myself to worry about rebuilding and repairing my relationship with them. Everything I did was about me, and only me. You know, I had this new life that I was going to make a go of, so I never even went to visit them without some kind of agenda. I went down there a few times when I needed money or when I was arguing with Johnny and needed to escape London. It was all very self-serving. I would turn up with Reggie, who was a problematic Staffordshire Bull Terrier, to say the least, and my dad would be like, 'What the fuck have you brought that dog here for?'

My dad was really proud of me when I got clean, but I was still holding it against him that he had said I deserved what I got. It made it easier for me to blame him for everything. It gave me a credit card of self-pity to hold against him, and I spent every last bit of that credit. I'd go on a massive fucking self-pitying shopping spree feeling sorry for myself. I had got to a point where I really did believe that everything I thought about people and my perception of things was absolutely true. I was consumed by it and the one thing or person I was most consumed by was my father.

Funny thing was, I had my tarot cards read when I came out of rehab, and the guy said that I was going to be close to my father. Of course, I told him that was never going to fucking happen, but the guy said to me, 'Your dad has the answers, he knows what's right.' Whatever, mate, you've got this wrong. And then, three months later, all this happens.

So, I had been in prison and was up in front of the judge for the bail hearing and my mum had written a letter saying I could be bailed to her house and stay there in Dungeness. I got out on the cash bail that Johnny and Del had borrowed from everyone, and suddenly at forty-two I was back living with my parents. In the middle of fucking nowhere, in the middle of winter, on a beach, freezing cold with nothing to do, sober. It was a fucking nightmare, but I had freedom. I was no longer in a police cell and I could fight my corner at last and I had a voice.

It was like starting all over again. I remember getting to the house and my dad just looked at me and said, 'What the fuck is going on?' And as I told him, he just looked at me and shook his head. It's not something you want to hear, is it? Your son's been a fucking mess for twenty-eight years and then, just as you think there's light at the end of the tunnel, that he's got himself clean and he's sorting himself out, this happens. He ends up in police custody. My dad was pretty much housebound by this point, he was in his seventies and could just about walk to the car and drive short distances, but that was about it. I remember for the first few days he was very rigid with me. You know, I was in his house and I was taking over, and I was under their feet. I had a blow-up bed in their front room and all of a sudden was just there in their space. Even I realised I was going to have to do everything I could to help to make this work. It was that or back to prison. Those were my options.

I'd treat him to fish and chips, go to the shops for them, take the dogs for a walk and do errands.

The police had my mobile phone so I had to go and get a new phone, and I had to get the money to get a new mobile (thanks Mum) and slowly and surely all the people who supported me came to visit. Del drove hours to come and visit me every week, as did my friend Bev, and Johnny brought the dogs down, which became my saving grace.

The thing, or should I say person, that my dad and I started bonding over, was my mum. She was our common ground and she was a fucking nightmare. I love her with all of my heart and she has stood by me through thick and thin, but fuck me, she does not shut up. She will nag you, and nag you, and nag you. 'Tony can you take the dog for a walk . . . when are you taking that dog for a walk?' When are you doing this, when are you doing that? Just little things, she would go on and on and on about, then it would turn into, 'How many times do I have to ask you to do this?' Then it would get to a point where I would answer her back, then: 'Don't you backchat me!' and before you knew it, my dad would be involved saying, 'Will you two fucking shut up!' She would nag my dad about anything and everything too – about his car, about the house, she just loved to moan. 'Mick,' I can hear her saying, 'when are you finishing painting that hallway?' I'm just the same. Her birthday is four days after mine and we just don't stop chipping away. I used to blame my dad for everything, but living there as an adult, I suddenly realised that my mum was just as fucking bad. When you're around them 24/7 you see it all in a different light. I saw my mum's planning and plotting and scheming. Her trying to go out shopping without my dad noticing and spending like it was going out of fashion. Again, I'm just the same.

Of course, it wasn't great that my father was pretty much housebound but it meant I really got to know him and he really got to know me. It turns out he wasn't the man I thought he was, he wasn't the dad that I wanted him to be. He was so much better. I wanted him to be that bastard, I wanted him to be that evil person, the one that said I deserved it. I wanted him to be the one that still got drunk. The one that would take it out on my mum and beat us with belts. But he wasn't that person anymore, and all of the things I held against him for years were circumstantial. Yes, as I child I thought he beat my mum up every weekend, but that wasn't the truth. He did beat my mum up, and he had his demons, but it was a few times a year, rather than every week as I believed, and as I had remembered for so, so many years. It still didn't make it right, and the trauma was awful, and yes, he had punished us the only way he knew how, and yes, he had a problem with booze, but he had sorted it out. My dad hadn't had a drink for thirty years by this stage, and he was so strong-willed. He stopped because he didn't like the person it turned him into.

He loved his cars, bless him, and I remember my mum had got him a brand-new Saab convertible and I'd ask him to drive me places and the response was always, 'For fuck's sake,' but he'd take me anyway. Everything was always a moan, but he would do it. I think that's where I get my grumpiness from, that's why everything is always a drama when it's not. So we'd go for mini drives – just to the shops or on errands, then we would sit there and watch TV together. My dad ruled the remote when it came to what was on the TV, except for *Coronation Street*, which my mum would watch every single night. And every night my dad would complain about it. 'Not this bloody shit again.' But if you asked him a question about what was going on in *Corrie*, he could tell you the answer straight away.

About a month into me living with them in Dungeness, I went up to London to see my lawyer. When I got back, my dad asked me what had happened. The evidence had come back and, well, there was no evidence. My dad told me I was being really strong and that he knew I'd done nothing wrong. I apologised to my dad whilst I was living down there. I sat down with him and I said, 'You know what, I'm so sorry for everything I've put you through.' And he turned around and said, 'Come back when you're six years clean.' And I was like, 'What?' And he said, 'Fuck off, and come back when you're six years clean and sober.' It wasn't about time. He meant, don't apologise until I knew what I was apologising for. I had no idea what I was really apologising for at that stage, and he was fucking right – again.

You see, when you come out of rehab and you're clean, you want to fix the world and tell everyone, 'I'm sorry, I'm sorry, I'm sorry.' But making amends isn't about telling people that you're sorry. It's about fixing the problems you've caused. Some amends that you make in life don't need to be vocalised, they just need to be done. You know, there are some situations that I've got myself into that can't be fixed, and could never be fixed, but what I can do is help others avoid getting into those situations. Which is what I do by working with different charities, it's a part of me making amends for the things I can't go back and fix.

My dad didn't live to see me stay clean for six years – he died five months after the court case ended. After I was cleared and had moved back to London, my friend Ezra would drive me down to Dungeness once a week and I would get the clippers out and trim my dad's beard for him. I'd go to the shop and get things for him like shoes and slippers. My dad had always been a big man, but towards the end of his life he had put on so much weight, by the time he died he was thirty-two stone. He had to sit and wear an oxygen mask in the evenings and the doctors used to give him exercise bands to use at home and he'd be like, 'What the fucking hell is this shit? You think I'm standing there like a cunt looking like a fucking idiot doing that?' I would tell him to shut up and do it, but it sounds exactly like something I would say now. At this stage, randomly, they had chicken coops in the back garden and I remember getting them some more chickens as a fox had got in and killed theirs. I said to my dad, 'You get the chickens and I'll give you the money.' He was like 'Yeah, yeah, sure. That old chestnut.' I mean, in all fairness to him, I had spent the last twenty-eight years never paying anyone a penny back.

I was shopping in Chelsea when I got a call from my mum. She was crying and saying that my dad was really ill and she thought he was dying. I thought she was being melodramatic as usual. She said that there was an ambulance there and he couldn't breathe and really needed to go to the hospital but wouldn't get in the ambulance. I was like, 'Put him on . . . Dad! What the fuck are you doing?' But still he refused to go, so I was like, 'Okay. I'll tell you what, I'm going to come down first thing in the morning and I will bring you the money for the chickens,' and he laughed and went, 'Yeah right, I'll believe that when I see it.' And I said, 'No, I'll be there, I'll bring the cash, we'll sort this out and then we can work out where you need to be, whether you need to go to the hospital or not,' and he was still like, 'No, I don't fucking need to go to hospital. I'll see you in the morning.' And that was it, that was the last conversation we ever had.

I went down the following morning, I was in the bank near their house and my mum rang me screaming and crying, saying, 'Your dad's dying, your dad's dying.' She didn't sound like she had the day before, I'd never heard my mum like this. We jumped back in the car and drove to the house, and as we got there he'd had a massive heart attack. Me and my mum held his hands, and we said our goodbyes to him and he passed. Ezra was with me, which I see as an act of a higher power, because he was a nurse and an ambulance driver and was there just when he was most needed.

His death hit my mum hard. She was devastated. I think she had been tied to my dad for so long, and towards the end, because he couldn't go out and do anything, he had become her complete life. My dad was big in every sense of the word, and his death left a massive void. But my mum's an incredibly strong woman, she's practical and pragmatic. I mean you'd have to be, dealing with us lot all her life. I remember us sitting down and sorting out the funeral, choosing a beautiful Gothic church in Lydd, deciding on the flowers and making sure all the people that should be there were there.

I was still no saint – I remember, even then, I had a grievance with my older brother, who was mourning too.

He'd just lost the only dad he'd ever had and I told the vicar that my dad had two sons and one adopted. I mean, how evil. I still held so much resentment towards him, and it was only later that I looked back at that and saw how wrong that was.

If it hadn't been for the court case, I would never have got that time with my father. Being down there was such a magical thing, because I got to know him again, and I was able to let go of this idea of who I thought he was. Even though his death was traumatic and it was awful seeing my mum go through that, and saying goodbye to her life partner of forty years, seeing my dad pass away was probably one of the most amazing things I'd ever experienced. Being able to be there when he died and be of service to my mum, and to him. I would never have had those moments if I hadn't got sober; I would never have had those moments without being posted to the house. I would never have been able to be there for them.

Even though we managed to turn our relationship around in the last year of his life, I still have so many regrets with my dad. I regret that I didn't listen to him. I regret that I didn't take the time to get to know who he was sooner. I regret that I was too consumed with using, and using him as an excuse to be who I was.

I remember my dad saying to me one night whilst I was staying with them, 'You know, I'm really proud of you, and I'm really proud of everything you've achieved.' And I was like, 'What?? What did you say?'

'You heard. I've said it once. I'm not going to say it again.'

Okay, Dad, I'll take that. Thank you.

17.

Don't Call It A Comeback

You see, the problem I had was that if I couldn't go back to DJ'ing, I didn't have any backup options. I had no qualifications. I didn't even have one fucking GCSE, all I had was a degree from the School of Life, a masters in MDMA with extra credits for triple dropping and smoking meth. I'd never had what you might call a proper job, so I had to make it work. I had to fall in love with music again. I had to make music my drug, not sex, not shopping or gossiping or any of those initial things I did when I first came out of treatment. They were my replacement highs but I needed to make music my drug of choice. The reason that first gig back at Too Too Much was so awful was because I hadn't yet reignited my love for music. Music had been the first and best drug of my life and it was really hard to get back into that. Slowly but surely, listening to music and remembering how much I loved it started to bring that back. I remember George coming to my house about eighteen months after I'd been clean. He had bought me one of those early white MacBooks as a present and I remember being like, *Oh my God, I can't believe I've got my own laptop*, because at the time – apart from a lot of front and bravado – I didn't have anything. That's when I really started to reconnect with music. When I get a new gadget or toy, I become obsessed – still do now – and this was no exception. I started to download music and kind of caught up with where music was at in the twenty-first century. You have to remember, before that, all I had was a load of chewed-up old CDs that I dragged around with me and before that, a bag of vinyl records. Music had moved on.

I'd never once contemplated the reality of having to go and get a real job, going to the Job Centre and doing interviews, or working somewhere like Sainsbury's or Tesco's. Never once. I thought I could be a club promoter and be relatively good at it. Also, in the back of my mind, I had what I considered an absolute stroke of genius. My fail-safe backup plan if I couldn't make a living from DJ'ing. Drum roll, please . . . I was going to be a sober drug dealer. All the dealers I'd known always had loads of cash and I knew it was a guaranteed way to make money, and a lot of it, and as I was sober I wouldn't be doing any of the drugs and eating, or sniffing, into the profits. I mean, my dealers had always made so much money from me that I could make a fortune. That was my brilliant backup career. In my warped mind, it was a fucking genius plan. It was that or become a really good, world-famous actor, obviously. Both completely fail-safe career options. I think I might have mentioned them to a few people and they were like, 'You're fucking mental, mate.' They might have had a point.

So really, I had no option but to get back behind the decks. I started playing gay clubs again because luckily I'd never really disappeared from that scene, and they were happy to take me back but I was still nervous as fuck. This was about three years in and I'd learned not to take things for granted again. I'd learned not to turn up and assume that things would just happen. I'd turn up at the gig and be telling myself, 'You can do this, you can do this.' I'd had anxiety before gigs before, but it had been anxiety like, 'Shit, can I see straight, can I walk straight?' or like, 'Fuck, I've been up for three days,' and the biggest anxiety of all – 'Will the dealer still be up at 4am on a Monday morning when I finish this gig?' Because in the old days I knew I had to do drugs to do the gigs, and to get drugs I had to get the gigs, and then to keep going I had to get drugs. I was on a cycle and it was exhausting. Now it was a case of DJ'ing sober and I had never done that before. I didn't know if I could – I hadn't ever played one track completely sober, even in the very early days I would have been pissed. It wasn't that I was nervous around drugs, at this stage I had a whole ring of Rottweilers around me who would protect me from that stuff. It was the anxiety that, when sober, I would just be a really shit DJ.

It was when they brought back the big Trade parties that I felt things starting to shift. I'd got a bit of confidence back and I'd bump into people and they'd say I should do something with them and then it just kind of started to filter back through and one thing would lead to another. I was living with Gina in Hampstead and he'd get me to do stuff for him and I'd get him to do stuff for me in return and it just started to build again. We started to work with the Hepatitis C trust together and did parties for them, and then Gina took me to David Furnish's birthday party, and that's when I got pally with him and Elton again – it all just grew organically.

When I played for Elton John in Nice a few years ago, that felt like a real moment. He and David have been very supportive. Elton flew me over to play the Troubadour Club in LA (which was where he broke America in the 70s) for the *Rocketman* premiere. That was insane. I've flown over and been to his Oscars party too, which always feels nuts. Someone asked me if I had to do a lot of work to get back into the US, meaning, wasn't it hard to get in with a drugs record? Believe it or not, I don't have a criminal record. I know, right? The time I was arrested at Heathrow I got off because it wasn't my jacket. It was a friend's I'd borrowed so I just said I didn't know it was in the sleeve pocket. You know, when the police stop homeless people, they don't arrest them, they just have to be seen to be going through the motions and I think it was a little bit of that, to be honest. I think they saw me walking along off my fucking nut and thought, *Jesus, we're not dealing with that.*

The next step up that I needed came when Annabel's threw their 50th Anniversary party in 2013. Bear in mind I'd been sober for six years by that point. It really did take a while for things to get going again. They'd got in touch with Kate and asked her to do the music but she didn't want to do it on her own. So we came up with Fat Moss. I'd been doing music for my mates for years and if she ever had a party I would play or I'd do her a playlist. We had done some DJ'ing before that together when I'd done the music with her for a Prada event. I knew the music she was into because we'd always been around each other from the early days. We've got very similar tastes in music, apart from the Rolling Stones, and it's great fun to bounce off each other on what tracks we were going to play. For

Annabel's, we wanted to play all of our favourite tracks –
'Ain't Nothing Going On But The Rent', 'MacArthur Park',
all the best bits from the 70s, 80s and 90s. It was at her
house in Highgate when we came up with Fat Moss. We
were there and trying to come up with a name, and it was
obvious – she'd always been rail thin and it was a laugh.

That night itself was insane, to me it felt like it came at
the end of an era of parties in London when nights and
people were truly wild, and the press were all over them
outside in a scrum. It was one of the last events at the old
Annabel's nightclub before they moved to the new venue,
and that place, the floors and the walls, were just soaked
in fun. We did it with Grace Jones, who was on first. She
was hula hooping as she always does and Kate crawled into
the hula hoop and Grace started trying to spank her with
her whip. It was fucking nuts. Then we came on and played
'MacArthur Park' to open and everyone went crazy. It really
felt like a pinch-me moment. I remember Harry Styles being
there just as he was the biggest thing going on in pop music
and dancing in front of the DJ booth all night. The Spice
Girl Mel B kept trying to come into the DJ booth and Kate
just told her to fuck off. A girl from Leeds should know
never to take on a supermodel from Croydon.

All of a sudden everyone wanted to book Fat Moss, we
were being booked to go everywhere. We went to Brazil to
AmFar, we were flown in by helicopter to open clubs in
Mykonos, Hong Kong – everywhere. When we were in Sao
Paulo in Brazil for AmFar, it was just insane. We went to
this guy's house and he had a fucking zoo in there. He's
one of two really famous brothers who live there, and they
had a shark hanging from the ceiling covered in diamanté.

Kylie Minogue came too and did a little set in the guy's nightclub in the basement. To have gone from being so, so on the outside, it felt like a really big breakthrough.

Then we were booked to do a gig in Mykonos where we played back-to-back old-school dance bangers. I love DJ'ing with a friend but it's a lot more fucking hassle. When I'm working, I call the shots and I do what I do. When there's two of you in the DJ booth, it totally changes the dynamic and it's twice the work, especially when they say, 'Play that doo, doo, doo one,' and you're like, 'What the fuck is that?!' That aside, me and Kate doing Fat Moss together was amazing. Kate as a friend is honest, she's caring, she's loving and she's so supportive – she's everything you could want from a friend – she really helped put me back on the map because that's what real friends do, they see the good in you and they want to see you shine. It was then that people who didn't know me from before started to pay attention – all of a sudden really mainstream brands and publications like the *Sunday Times Style* were booking me to play parties.

It was when I was in Cannes to do a Fashion for Relief gala with Naomi Campbell that I remember getting to the Martinez Hotel and thinking, *Wow, is this going to be my life now?* It's one of the biggest hotels there where everyone stays and does press junkets for the film festival and it just felt like a real moment. Remember, there had been times not so long before that I'd been essentially homeless going from friend's to friend's with a carrier bag of belongings. Anyway, we were doing Fashion for Relief and DJ Mos, who is a big DJ from New York, was there. I'd heard that Mary J Blige was performing and, of course, I'd been obsessed with her song 'No More Drama' – I was going to have it played at my funeral. This was to be one of the first big international gigs I'd played since I got clean. Before I got sober I was never starstruck, the bravado of drink and drugs just carried me through. But this was different. Suddenly, I was really nervous and I really wanted to meet Mary J Blige.

Anyway, I told DJ Mos the story and he was like, 'You have to tell her.' So he went to get her and I told her about me playing her song every day on repeat and that it was the song I was going to have played at my funeral as the curtains closed and my body went in to be cremated. I mean, I'm amazed she didn't just think I was some kind of nut job and make a swift exit, but I told her some of my story, and she was like, 'Wow,' and started crying. Can you fucking believe it? Mary J Blige was crying because of my story. She said, 'I can see your aura, the person in front of me is who you're meant to be and your story has really touched me.' It was a really spiritual moment of my life that reaffirmed a lot for me . . . The fact that the words to the song meant as much to her as they did to me. The fact that she'd been so lovely to me when she could have been so dismissive. I thought she was an old-school diva – kind of like me – but she'd been so humble. What a life lesson to learn. She requested me to do two parties with her after that.

Reconnecting with Edward Enninful, British *Vogue* editor-in-chief, definitely felt like the act of a higher power, in so much of what it represented to me. I'd known Edward for years, way back from when he was eighteen and out on the London club scene and at *i-D* magazine. Before he got the *Vogue* job, the British Fashion Council awarded him with the Visionary of the Year award, and so we did an after-party at the Café Royal. The party was in the Oscar Wilde room – named after their most famous patron – and it was all going off. I remember Kate was in one corner, and Rihanna in another with all of her gang, and as the party came to an end Rihanna offered me £5k on the spot for us to take the decks to her suite upstairs and carry on playing. I said no, which felt like a real achievement. Remember, I'm the guy who could never stop, but even though the party had been brilliant, it was time to call it a night. I'd had twenty-eight years of never having done that, not once.

The next party I did for Edward was his OBE party at Mark's Club in London, where everyone went wild. Mark's Club is this grand old members' club in Mayfair. Everything in there is worth a fortune and we had people dancing on these antique chairs and sofas with Madonna right next to the DJ booth. I went in to see Edward and the team at Condé Nast in Hanover Square after that and he asked me to be *Vogue*'s resident DJ. Edward is another one who has been there from the start – loving and supportive. Edward is fun, loves music and he's never changed – people see the serious side because of his job, but there's a really fun side to him too and I just love him. The last time I had been at Vogue House was before I went to rehab and I'd been picking fag butts out of the ashtrays. To go to doing playlists for *Vogue*, writing for them and being their in-house DJ, was such a major example of going from the outside to the inside. You know, DJ'ing at Marc Jacobs' wedding in New York was major. Playing in Donatella Versace's front room was pretty epic. Playing for Victoria Beckham and her asking me to play 'Spice Up your Life' while she brought on a drag tribute act to the Spice Girls was genius. Considering her public persona for so many years was dry as old bones and moody, in real life, she's fucking hilarious. She's got such a dry sense of humour that's a laugh a minute. Like Elton and David, Victoria and David Beckham have been fiercely loyal and have booked me for everything they've done. You know, at the end of the day, I must be a good fucking sober DJ.

Playing the Serpentine Summer Party, which is one of the biggest events on the fashion and social calendar in the UK, was a really big moment for me. I did the Serpentine's two annual events that day. The first was the committee's party in the afternoon where the London Mayor Sadiq Khan made a speech – I wanted to throw something at his head. I mean, the man has single-handedly done more to destroy London than anyone else in the city – have you tried to get from one side of London to the other in under a month? Anyway, then I did the really big glitzy number in the evening where literally anyone who's anyone attends. They had built this huge red cube on the stage as part of that year's installation and it spun around me as I played. So there I was, playing inside this box which is moving around in front of everyone major in London.

When I get super-stressed, nervous and feel the pressure, or when I'm tired, I gurn. A lot of people can't get their heads around it and automatically assume that I've had some kind of relapse. It's actually from where the neural pathways in my brain were so fucking shot that when I'm in a situation I associate with drink and drugs, I will sometimes gurn like a motherfucker who's just double-dropped. The first gig I did after rehab, everyone thought I was using again, and I've had to do serious work on righting those neural pathways. Now, if I'm doing a big gig, I put my tongue on pressure points in my mouth to stop it, so it's very rare that you'll see me gurning, but if you know me, you'll be able to tell if I'm stressed at a gig if you see my jaw going as I'm DJ'ing – and that's after fifteen years of being clean. There are other examples too – I used to love doing a line and then going shopping. Oh my God, it was one of my favourite things. And even now, sometimes if I'm out shopping and going into the changing rooms, I'll feel my nose dripping. Seriously.

People ask what the biggest gig of my life has been and I like to say it hasn't happened yet. People ask me what the best club I've ever been to is, and I tell them I've never been there. Every job is different. I'm very privileged in that I no longer believe the hype of what I do. I'd love to be in a position where I didn't think that I looked old or fat, or I didn't worry that people are going to hate my music. But all of that makes me push myself. I sit in the back of taxis praying on the way to work now because if I keep that negativity in my head then I fuck up. It's a hard thing to explain to someone who's never experienced low self-esteem, because it is a real contradiction in itself. You want to do well, and that low self-esteem means that you push yourself to do well, but then when you get there, you feel like you don't deserve it and there's a part of you that wants to sabotage it. I don't listen to that voice anymore, but I do sit there worrying that people aren't going to turn up. I did a gig recently that was completely sold out and still, I just couldn't accept that the place was sold out because people wanted to come and see me.

I haven't taken a moment for granted this time around.

I feel like a lottery winner, like I don't belong or deserve to be here, whether it's on the stage playing for people, or being paid to fly around in the name of work.

I've gone from people ignoring me in the street because I had no teeth and I looked like I was dying to people coming up and wanting to have their picture taken with me.

And you know, it's taken me a lifetime to get here.

THINGS I'VE LEARNED FROM SOCIAL MEDIA

Be as blunt and honest as possible – it makes the idiots run
for the hills. No one likes to be confronted with their own
truths.

As Joan Rivers always said, 'Never be afraid to laugh at
yourself. After all, you could be missing out on the joke of
the century.' I can laugh at the drugs stuff on social media
because I've lived it. I've lived that pain and now I can see
the lightness.

I've learned the fewer filters I have, the fewer filters I need.
Because I have everything out there, I don't need protecting
– I have no skeletons in my closet.

Social media is a great tool to teach you to accept praise.

You put down drink and drugs and suddenly discover the
biggest drug of all – Instagram.

Be careful how you use social media. Social media use is
great. Social media abuse isn't. Know your limits.

Always remember that social media is not real life.

Instagram is not QVC. Remember that.
You know who you are . . .

If someone's trying to pick a fight with you on social media
then as my once friend Naomi says, 'Just play dead.'

Social media is all about timing. Don't feel like you need
to put everything up straight away. Store stuff and remember
to live in the moment.

Above all else on social media, remember that you need to be a bloody good thief. I don't complain about anyone posting my memes as I nick loads as well. 'Can you credit me?' Do I look like a fucking bank?

18.
Redemption

It's a fair question to ask someone what they do with their days after they've spent twenty-eight years in pursuit of pure hedonistic pleasure. A third of a lifetime bouncing from eight-ball to eight-ball, disco to dick, and then . . .? Leaves a bit of time on your hands, doesn't it? Well, you start to give back. Because the thing about addiction is, it doesn't discriminate. It doesn't care if you're a sex worker or a superstar, whether you grew up on a council estate in Battersea or a mansion in Belgravia. I've worked with everyone from the homeless to household names and giving back is what keeps me clean. I've never once seen someone having fun at a party, judged them, and called them up the next day and said that they needed to stop, because you can't tell people not to have fun. But, if I see someone struggling, or they ask me for help, then I will intervene. I've had people calling me and saying that they're about to kill themselves, or that their partner has just tried to commit suicide, and asking if I could go and see them at the Nightingale Hospital, which specialises in mental health, to meet them. I've gone into plenty of psychiatric wards before now. I've done the rounds.

I like to argue that I started helping people the day I left treatment, course I do, but it's actually true in a lot of ways, because people come to you and say, 'Oh, wow, you're clean now, how did you do it?' It really is as simple as that – telling them how you got clean. By leading by example, people see that you've got your sparkle back and they see the change in you and they think, *Oh, if he can do it then I can do it, too.* What you have to remember is that I was so far gone that no one ever thought that I would – or could – do it. I had one fucking tooth left and looked like I'd been dead for a year, for fuck's sake, and when the people that were still on the scene saw me sticking to sobriety, it was a bit of a moment. Seriously, if I could turn it around then anyone could.

But, it was around 2010 when I officially started helping. I'd been in recovery for a few years and my dad had died and when I'd done enough work on myself, I felt I needed to find a new purpose in life. You have to do the twelve steps, and normally by the time you get to about the sixth step you might be ready to be a sponsor. A sponsor is someone who takes on someone new to recovery, leads by example, helps them and gives them advice and support.

The big shift for me came when I really learned to care about myself. I'd had thirty years of hating myself and going from person to person, using them and completely sucking them dry. When I stopped that, when I had that shift of being able to love myself, I was able to start loving other people. I'd had thirty years of destruction, and just survival, and there's a big difference between surviving and living. Once you learn that, everything changes.

When I first started sponsoring, I would find it incredibly

hard getting close to someone, looking after them, building a close relationship with them and then letting them go. The relationship continues, but they get to a stage where they just don't need you as much anymore, or at least that's the stage you pray they'll get to. When someone comes to me for help, I put so much energy into it that they almost become like my kid. When someone really needs you, you'll check in on them every day or even a few times a day to make sure they're all right, then when they're getting better and working on themselves, they'll start to need you less and less.

You do get attached to people because you spend so much time with them, but you have to get to a point where, like a parent, you let go. But those are the success stories – that's what you want to happen, that's why you're always on the end of the phone. But there are those who don't make it, who relapse and then just disappear. I had a little guy who became a really close friend and I gave him a job and he would come to my house every day and we were really making progress, but then one day he relapsed and was gone – that was four years ago. He's still alive but he's lost in a life of G (GHB, which is a synthetic drug, like a liquid form of Ecstasy), crystal meth and prostitution. He was such a sweet guy, and it's really awful, it's such a sad life. Those drugs destroy people, especially meth – it switches people's brains off. Meth is talked about so little in the UK. It's still the drug of shame.

The first people to really take me back, in terms of work anyway, had been the big club owners, people like Laurence Malice who owned the Egg and used to run Trade, and Lee Freeman who ran nights like Fiction and DTPM. They had never really turned their backs on me and had always made it clear that the door would be left open. So, when I was ready, I found myself working in a gay after-hours club in Vauxhall, which ran from the early hours of the morning and generally kept running throughout the weekend. It had been one of my favourite playgrounds when I was in the depths of my addiction.

Being sober and back on that scene was like walking into the fucking Crimean War, there were so many casualties. There would be hundreds of people lying on the floor in tinfoil blankets all overdosed on G with nowhere for any of them to go. If you're not familiar, G – which as I mentioned is like a liquid form of Ecstasy – is a drug which the gays love because it never burns muscle mass, even if you're out dancing for three days, and it's great for sex. Problem is, it's so, so addictive, and dangerous to take – if you mix it with alcohol or take too much then you can slip into a coma and die.

G had been around for a little while but then crystal meth hit London big time and the combination of the two drugs made guys want to fuck like rabbits, and the Chemsex scene flared up. It was a scene no one was talking about. Like I said, if someone is having fun, I would never intervene, but these drugs are so powerful that people were becoming lost in them. I decided to put my head above the parapet and went on Channel 4 News and spoke about it. I got so much hate mail from my own community when I did that. I had poked a new hole in their gayness and spoken about something that they would have preferred to stay hidden. But so many people were destroying their lives in that world – they were the people I was trying to help, like I said –

I've never called anyone out who was really having fun and handling it.

With the queer community, no one thinks that they have a problem because that's just what we do. When we're young and we get introduced to gay culture, suddenly we're submerged into it and take on this persona, and that's what we think gay culture is all about. You come to London or you go into any gay scene and everyone goes, 'Oh, this is what we do on the gay scene. We take loads of drugs. We go and party. We do crystal meth, we do G and this, and this, and you know we end up at sex parties.' And very quickly you can take on that persona and get swept away by it.

At that point in time, when the whole Chemsex thing was going on, people really weren't voicing their concerns about what was happening, and it was ruining lives. Like I said, addiction doesn't discriminate on the basis of class or career, and it doesn't discriminate against education either. It couldn't give a fuck if you've got a double first from Oxford. Because crystal meth wasn't a street drug, when it arrived in the UK there weren't labs here making it so everything was being imported and it was expensive and it was starting to become a bit of, 'Oh, look what the gays are doing again.' The majority of people using crystal meth then were professionals. They were people with money – doctors, lawyers – because it's not a street drug, and it's more addictive than heroin. Something the dealer won't mention when he's giving you the bag.

Suddenly everyone was doing it without realising just how dangerous a drug it was. The majority of my friends who were professional and doing it just couldn't admit they had a problem. So as soon as you go out there and start saying, 'Okay, there's a hidden epidemic here, and no one's talking about it because there are no stats,' then you're putting yourself in the firing line. No one was getting arrested for crystal meth. No one was getting arrested for carrying G on them because the police didn't know what G was.

So, I was out there talking about G and the fact that there was going to be a pandemic and no one was listening. And suddenly G started being available online as a drain cleaner and all of a sudden these young kids started taking it. Then people started to open their eyes because suddenly, it was their kid, their straight son who was addicted to GHB. Suddenly, it was mainstream, and the same happened with crystal meth – a gang flooded Dublin with it, and it took hold of the whole city. No one was doing coke or crack – just crystal – and it made headline news because, you know what? It makes straight guys and girls want to fuck like bunnies, too. Addiction doesn't differentiate between sex or sexuality.

Another big problem was that you could go onto apps like Grindr and people would put 'chems' on their profile. So we started canvassing them. Dave Stuart, who sadly recently passed away and worked at 56 Dean Street, the sexual health centre in Soho, and myself had a chat and tried to work out what we could do. We sent emails to the sites saying, 'Look, you need to stop this. There are people openly selling drugs on your app.' And they just ignored it. That's how I ended up with Jon Snow talking about barebacking on the fucking seven o'clock Channel 4 News. You have to watch it. I was nervous as fuck, I had my first proper set of teeth in. I'm not sure Jon Snow had ever heard of barebacking or crystal meth before, but, you know, you learn something new every day.

Our biggest breakthrough came when I was away on holiday with some model friends in Mykonos, and the owner of Grindr was at the same beach club as us one day and wanted to meet them. So I introduced him, and at the same time, I said, 'You do realise you're responsible for drug dealing on your app?' And he was like, 'What do you mean?' I said, 'The word "chem" is so freely put on there. If I put an erect penis on my profile, it'd be removed in three seconds and yet you allow people to sell drugs openly and to anybody on there.' About three days later, they changed the rules and finally put a stop to it. It just took a conversation at the right time, in the right place, to make it happen. The universe sometimes works like that.

But, there was still a problem.

Here's a little lesson on drug dependency, so settle down and listen up. There are dependent drugs and interdependent drugs. Dependent drugs are those that the body needs to be weaned off: heroin, alcohol and GHB are amongst these. Interdependent drugs are those which the body has a psychological dependency on – these include weed, cocaine and crystal meth. The difference being that you can go cold turkey on interdependent drugs without having to be physically weaned off them, and while the hell is still the same, you won't cause yourself any physical damage. However, if you try to go cold on dependent drugs then there are many things that can go very wrong. That was what was happening with G users. There were kids in their early twenties hooked on it and taking it on the hour and then having heart attacks and dying in police custody from withdrawal. No one was educated about it or had any idea – the police hadn't been trained on what to look for with G, and GHB doesn't stay in the system long enough to show up in an autopsy, so the causes of death kept being recorded as heart failure. My friend Tommy and I went in and spoke to the police, and we trained them. Then we set about canvassing rehab clinics. I went back to Arlington House and taught them about 'Gay Lifestyle Issues'. The word Chemsex has been used quite freely and it was such a dirty word. To be clear, it's not like we were trying to give Chemsex a rebrand, it was and is what it is. You know, there was a real shame attached to it, and it was a lifestyle issue, so we set about trying to take the stigma away from it, and making it more acceptable to talk about, canvassing rehabs and working it into their programmes. I went to a place called City Roads – a detox centre in Islington – to talk to them about G and say, 'Listen, this is what's going to be coming through your doors.' They had no clue because up to that point, it was all about alcohol and heroin. There were all these amazing treatment centres in England that had been open for years and they'd all been trained and were great at dealing with alcohol, cocaine, crack and heroin addiction, but not crystal meth and G.

We were doing talks and going around the major drug conferences, organisations like ACAS, who give employment advice to employers and employees and these big pharmaceutical companies that were getting me to go and talk about what was coming through on the scene. We went over to Thailand and set up Resort 12. This was an LGBTQ+ treatment centre, run by the LGBTQ+ community for – but by no means exclusively for – the LGBTQ+ community. We wanted to create a safe space where there was no stigma attached to any gay lifestyle issues, where you could be open and say anything without feeling shame. It was a treatment centre run by people who had been through this stuff and knew how to treat it. This is a programme like no other, a one-stop shop for gays. The way I looked at it was, no one knew our community like our community, and treatment centres were trying but getting it wrong with guys with crystal meth issues. You know, you've got to understand gay lifestyle issues to deal with gay lifestyle issues. So, what we did with Resort 12 was to make a safe place for people from all around the world that had problems, whether it be sex addiction, crystal meth, G or any form of addiction. And it wasn't just for the LGBQT+ community, either – its openness and freshness made it appealing to a very young demographic, too.

It was through Resort 12 that I met Barney. Barney has been my biggest heartbreak out of everyone I've come into contact with in recovery, by far. Every kid is special, but I remember Barney coming up to me after I'd shared my story at a group session at the rehab. I had told them all my worst gay shit, and here he was, this little nineteen-year-old straight boy coming up to this older gay guy who's just sat there and talked about pulling his teeth out, about sex addiction, shagging ten guys a day, and about my twenty-eight years of trying to destroy myself, and he comes and asks me to sponsor him. For him to come up to me afterwards, and say that he admired my honesty, and me sharing my truth, meant a lot.

So I took him on as my sponsee when we got back to the UK, and we started to work together, and for a little while it worked. I remember speaking to him and he just said, 'I can't do this anymore, Tony, I'm going to beat it.' He was really trying, and I was really trying to help him. But he was such a young kid, and he didn't get it, he just wasn't ready. Because, that's another thing – addiction doesn't discriminate against age, either.

I remember speaking to him on the Thursday night and he said he was struggling. I was like, 'Okay, well you need to get to a meeting tomorrow and talk about it,' and he said he would and that his friend was going to pick him up and take him to the meeting, so he called me before and he went, and then called me after from McDonald's, and told me he was going to use that night. I just remember saying, 'I can't keep doing this with you, Barney, you either want it or you don't.' He said that the meetings weren't working and that he needed to go back to rehab. I told him that he couldn't, he had already been twice, and had completely exhausted his parents' money. They weren't rich and they couldn't afford to keep sending him back there over and over again.

He had it in his head that he'd be going back to hang out with his mates, but all of the people he'd been in treatment with had gone. The rehab he thought he was going back to was completely different by then. Our conversation was turning into a row so I ended the call saying that I was going to go and that I would speak to him in the morning. Two minutes later he messaged and said, 'I'm going to get this, Tony, I'm going to do it. I'll call you in the morning.' He sounded so determined to get with the programme and beat the drugs, and I knew he meant it.

The next day I didn't hear from him, and I called and

texted and I called again. At about 5pm I got a call to say that Barney had passed away that morning. An overdose of ketamine.

The news completely annihilated me. I questioned if I'd been too tough on him. I questioned my own recovery. I started questioning whether helping people was what I wanted to do, and whether I could go through that again. It really threw me. But I don't think I would have said anything differently, he needed to hear those words, and the fact that he messaged me back and said he was going to do it, meant that I was getting through. I still have all of our messages on my phone and I've read them so, so many times. Getting that call was devastating. It really ripped my soul out. He was a very special kid.

That weekend, I had to do a talk in front of 3,000 people at a 12-step convention at the old Friends House on the Euston Road. It was too late to cancel so it was a matter of game face and jazz hands. I remember sitting on the stage on auto-pilot, pulling out the old gags and anecdotes and making people laugh, and then I came right up to date and spoke about Barney and I started sobbing on stage. For a long time it made me think that I couldn't sponsor anyone again, I just didn't know if I could carry on with it. I was sponsoring three others at the time, and I questioned whether I should find them new sponsors. But you have a responsibility to them, and you have a responsibility to yourself to get back up. That's addiction. That is what it does – every day is a battle, and if you lose that battle, you relapse.

What many people forget is that if they haven't taken drugs for six, seven months and they start using again, the body hasn't got the same resilience anymore. You start taking the same amount, because you're an addict and because you're a greedy fucking cunt, and the body can't handle it and your organs start to shut down and you overdose and die. It's a well-known statistic within the treatment world that only one in twelve people who go to rehab manage to stay in recovery long-term. That doesn't mean the other eleven die, but most will have relapses. You know, when it works it works. I'm living proof of that. If I can stop and start going to meetings and being honest – then anyone can. But for the other eleven, it can be heartbreaking. There's a lot more education to be done on addiction, there's still a lot left to do.

Barney was the first and only person who has died in my care. People had relapsed before and sometimes you just don't hear from them again – you reach out but they don't want it. Then you might hear later down the line that 'So-and-so has died'. But I'd never had it that close before, someone that I was supposed to be helping. I questioned what I'd done wrong, what could I have done to save him? For months and months afterwards I would wake in the middle of the night and not be able to sleep thinking about him and replaying that last conversation. The loss of Barney still haunts me – the fact that he was only nineteen and such a great kid. His mum is special too and now helps kids with addiction. Her strength alone restores my faith in the work I do, and the value of helping people. The fact that she now works to try and stop what happened to Barney happening to anyone else is so inspiring.

I wish I could react differently to people not doing what I want them to do, but sometimes you have to let go of it.

No matter how much you see yourself in someone, it's not about you. It's about them destroying themselves, they wrestle alone in the dark, and you kind of need to let them do that, you can't chain them up and keep them prisoner to get them to stick with it. I sponsor six people at the moment, but I don't deal with them all every day. They get to about step 4 and you have to start letting them do their own thing, and trust them to get on with the work.

There are some people on this planet – and I know this is hard for most addicts, or anyone with slightly addictive tendencies to understand – but there some lucky fuckers who can go out and take drugs and have fun and know when to stop. I just don't get it – people who, after a bottle or two of wine at dinner go, 'Oooh, you know what I've got at home? I've got a gram left over from Christmas.' I mean. What. The. Actual. Fuck. Seriously?! 'I've got nine pills in my make-up bag left from Glastonbury last summer.' Fuck right off. I just don't get it – what? You fucking freak. How could you have anything left over? If I'd had nine pills left, I'd have said, 'Let's poke one up our bum, swallow another and snort one for good measure . . . or we could do a double drop, or a double poke – your call. Heads or tails?' But I definitely would not have had anything left. No one ever would when I was around.

But, like I said, there are some people who can just leave it sitting there.

And, you know what, good for them.

Lucky fucking bastards.

THINGS I'VE LEARNED FROM MUSIC

I've learned so much from music. I've learned empathy, I've learned feeling. Music isn't really about listening, it's about feeling. You really have to feel music to get it.

Music is your very own time machine. It has the power to transport you back to places and back to people that may no longer be with us. Nothing else can do that for you.

Music taught me that if you have a good record collection, you'll never be lonely.

I learned that if you close your eyes and open your ears to music, it really is a magical thing.

Music has no genre. You know, these DJ's that say they only play techno. Tech no notice. Whatever the genre, it has the ability to move you.

I learned how to live through music. There are certain songs and lyrics that have changed the path of my life. If you can sit through a George Michael album from start to end and not be moved, then you've not listened to it properly. Or you've got serious problems.

I learned that there's no such thing as 'cool' from music. No one wants to admit they're listening to the Spice Girls, but if that makes you happy, then there's nothing wrong with that.

I learned that if you put Magic FM on for a day, as cheesy as it is, you'll be in a better mood by the end of it.

I learned that, even after all those drugs, nothing can change the way I feel like music can.

19.

Success

I'd really love to end this book by saying that every day is blue skies, rainbows, glitter and unicorns. Although I hate unicorns – fucking stupid cunts. But, you know, life on life's terms is hard when you don't have anything to escape with. It's not all shits and giggles, but it is what you make of it. Now, if I have a bad day, I'll remember that it's just that – a day. Tomorrow will be a new one and it's not the end of the world.

People ask me if there's anything I would have done differently over the last fifty-odd years. I always like to say that I wouldn't change a thing, but that's a lie. I wish I'd listened, and who knows, maybe I should have taken some requests. When people tell you they need a word with you, that you're out of control – it's kind of a warning, right? I have no idea who the first person to take me to one side was, I mean . . . it was a long time ago and even then there was a massive fucking queue. But when your dealer is telling you that you're doing too many drugs, you know you've got a problem, right? I would just get another dealer on the side so that neither would know how much I was doing. I remember going to a gay sauna after we'd been clubbing with a friend and they turned me away at the door because they said I was too high. I mean, I did have my shoes in my hands at the time, but when you're being turned away from places like that, you have to wonder, don't you? I never saw any of it as any kind of warning or paid attention to anyone. I always saw it as jealousy. Jealous of me having fun, jealous of me doing what I was doing, and jealous that they didn't have my life.

I regret so much stuff I did, but if I was to dwell on everything I'd done, I'd never leave the house. I can't change what I've done. What I can do is try to make amends, I can apologise, but an apology is worthless unless you really mean it. And even apologies aren't always smooth sailing. I remember apologising to Patsy – I'd been one year clean and I bumped into him at a party and I really owed him an apology, but I didn't even know what I was apologising for. What counts is making sure it doesn't happen again. My past behaviour doesn't sit well with me. The problem I have is that if I'm with a group of people and someone's being bitchy, it's in my DNA that I have to be the bitchiest, I have to be the best. I can't help it, it's how I'm wired. But then an hour later my programme kicks in and I'll feel like shit, thinking, *Why on earth did I behave like that?*

What I can change is how I am today, how I behave and how I treat myself and others. If I'm honest, I have to work so hard to keep that side of me in check. No one, not me, you or anyone else, needs to see the side of me being a cunt. I posted a picture of me on Instagram at the depths of my addiction, and another picture of me sixteen years on, and it got 50,000 likes and 4,000 lovely comments.

That's the side of Tony I need to show. Back when I was an addict, I had the excuse that I wasn't in control. That it wasn't my fault. Now, it's completely on me so when I have my hissy diva fits, later on I think, *That's just not cool – you could have handled yourself so much better.* I've always been a reactor rather than an actor and my go-to defence mechanism is to use my bad behaviour like a loaded gun. So much of that behaviour, of being a complete and utter arse, was a way of avoiding any kind of real intimacy. I couldn't let anyone see how fucking scared I was.

How do I view that person now, the old Fat Tony? What a fucking nightmare. What. An. Absolute. Fucking. Nightmare. It's easier to laugh about stuff than to really dig deep and deal with it. But I am, and I will continue to. That behaviour is no badge of honour. Yes, it can be funny to read about and makes for great anecdotes – that's partly why it's in this book – but it's not something I'm proud of. It was truly terrible. Do I have compassion for the old Tony? Of course I do, he was so fucking lost, man. Of course he was going to be a cunt. He didn't know who he was. He had no identity so he had to make one, he either had to make you scared shitless or love him because he was the biggest cunt in the room making everyone laugh at someone else's expense. I really was the court jester, wearing ridiculous, expensive clothes. George used to say to me, 'Who the fuck are you entertaining?' Who *was* I entertaining? Why was I doing that? That Tony has my utmost compassion because he was just so lost.

There have been times when I've woken up in the night and wondered why I'm writing this book, why I'm airing my dirty laundry in public, why I'm putting everything out there, inviting people to judge me – which, in a way, I'm asking people to do. I'm in a good place right now, one I've worked so hard to get to, so why risk ruining it? And the answer to that is because if there's something in this book which helps just one person then it's all worth it . . . so, judge away.

Like all of us, I'm a work in progress, and will continue to be. So much has changed, like how I view success. For me, now, success is freedom. Freedom from addiction, from obsessive thoughts – that's success on a daily basis. Success is being able to go to bed at night knowing you've done some good that day. Knowing that your side of the street is clean. Success is self-respect because, to be respected by others, first you have to respect yourself. Success is being able to love yourself and being able to love others. Success is having a really strong friendship group and knowing that you have people to reach out to and who will reach out to you. Those are the building blocks of success. Love, wealth, career success, everything else comes from those foundations.

I've learned that success is subjective. The smallest win might be the biggest success you've ever achieved, and you must remember to enjoy that and be in the moment. People often remark how the last few years have been amazing for me in terms of my career. The way I see it, the minute I stopped taking drink and drugs was the day success started, and now it grows bit by bit, and blossoms in different areas of my life. Right now, it's my career, for which I'm very, very grateful.

I was sitting outside a restaurant having dinner recently and three people came up to me and said how they love what I do. I said thank you and took pictures with them.

Before I'd have been like, *Ooh, God*, and the compliments would have embarrassed me. Now, I realise how lucky I am that people are still interested in what I'm doing.

What have I learned? I've learned survival skills, life skills, and I've learned that I don't need things and places to make me happy. Lockdown served as a real opportunity for me to take a deep breath and get back to the simple things in life. I don't need to be spending £1,000 a week on taxis – that's obscene – I don't need to spend vast amounts of money on clothes that are only going to be worn a few times. That's not cool. Lockdown reminded me that I am enough. Don't get me wrong, I love nice clothes, and nice food, and nice restaurants, but they don't define who I am.

The pandemic reminded me that I can't fix the world but if I start to fix myself, it's a very good springboard. It taught me that, when my back's against the wall, that's when I become my most creative. You know, during lockdown I started a clothing line, I set up decks in my garden and started live-streaming, right at the very beginning when we didn't know how long it was going to go on for. I'd been posting things on Instagram for years, but just before lockdown I'd made a mini-documentary with a magazine called *MixMag*, which racked up over six million views. All of a sudden the documentary, my Instagram and the DJ sets from my back garden came together and people wanted to hear my story, and in part, it encouraged me to write this book.

People were losing their freedom, their jobs, their homes, and their loved ones so I kind of thought, *Okay, I'm just going to carry on being me*. Carry on posting inappropriate jokes, stealing everyone else's memes, and I'll put it all together in one place for people like a library, because that's what it is – a library that people can hopefully look at and laugh at.

The first time I heard about Instagram, I was in Ibiza with an old raver friend, probably about five years into being clean. Some kids were telling us about it around the hotel pool and we were like, 'What?!? What the fuck are you on about? So you set up an account and then you get an instant gram? How does that work? Fucking hell. Sounds amazing. Couldn't do that in the 80s.' I didn't get it at first, why would anyone want to put pictures up there of what they were eating or drinking or where they were staying? I remember the first video I saw when I suddenly realised I could get into it – it was a girl ricocheting down some stairs pissed and managing to lose her shoes but still get back up with her drink in her hand at the bottom. Then I was like, *Oh, these are my people. I can do that.*

My humour is there because there have been so many moments in my life when I have woken up and thought to myself, *Why the fuck did you do that? Why did you say that? Why did you make that call? Why did you push that person down the stairs? Why did you start a fight with the cab driver? Why did you steal everyone's money? Why did you take all their drugs?* All of these things I used to do and think that I was funny doing them. And you know what, it wasn't funny, but the reason I can laugh at those things now is because I've dealt with that past and I don't do that stuff anymore. A big part of my Instagram memes are drug-related because I've dealt with that past and I can laugh at it.

One of the biggest things I've learned is self-respect. You know, mental health is not just about the state of your mind, it's also affected by what you do, where you are, who you're spending time with and what you're eating. Take one of those out of the equation and you can go off balance. I spent twenty-eight years completely and utterly unbalanced. Sixteen years on, I've learned to manage myself pretty well. But it isn't just drink and drugs that can tip the scales, it can be working too much, not getting enough sleep, having too much sugar.

I've learned that recovery is an ongoing process and to try not to fast-forward everything and rush ahead. I've learned that it's okay to live in the now. It's taken me years of being clean to realise that. I've learned that it all starts with what's going on inside. Once you get your head sorted out, everything else falls into place around it. There's no way I could be working now and doing what I do without having those things in place.

These days, nothing gets me high like music does, I get that buzz every time I go to work. I don't take anything for granted anymore, every gig I go to I pray on the way that I'm going to do a good job. I don't go there and think, *Let's get this out of the fucking way*, anymore, every gig is like playing Madison Square Gardens, however many people are there. I'm doing my job, I'm doing what I love, and that's a fucking amazing thing.

To still be invited to play for big crowds and be at the top of my game at fifty-six is incredible and I don't take a moment of it for granted anymore. I was homeless, I had no teeth, I was fucking dying, and now I'm in a different world, and that is down to not taking drink, not taking drugs, finally listening and finally accepting that the work starts with me, and putting the time in. I'm so blessed, and I appreciate that all the time now. I don't ever get too comfortable. Nothing worth having in life ever comes from being comfortable – I'd rather run for a bus in six-inch heels than be sat in the back of a limousine.

I've learned how to tell the difference between use and abuse when it comes to alcohol, drugs, food, shopping. Anything. Sometimes when we think we're having a party, the party is actually having us. You know, no cocaine is ever as good as the first few lines of cocaine, and then you end up being a hoover for twenty-eight years. You're sucking up the same old shit on rotation. I would say to anyone, if you find yourself in trouble or think you might be in trouble, then speak out, because if you don't open your mouth, you don't get fed. It's as simple as that. If you've got a problem, voice it, don't hold onto it, because that problem will turn into another problem, and before you know it, you've got ninety-nine problems.

What would I say to my younger self? Shut up. It's as simple as that. Shut. The. Fuck. Up. I got clean and I still didn't shut up and listen. I have uncommon sense. Most people have common sense, where they know they need to go to the airport at 6am the next morning so they go to bed at 10pm the night before. I'd go out until 5am and then go home and go to the airport, it's just the way I'm wired. If you give me two options, I'll always choose the harder one. If you ask me if I want to run through a field of flowers or a field of glass, I'll choose the field of glass, even now, even in recovery. I'll cut myself to ribbons and then at the end maybe, just maybe, think that it's not working and maybe I should change. That's just the way it is. That's always the way it's been.

What have I learned about love? The biggest thing I've

learned about love is that you have to love yourself before you can love anyone else. As clichéd as it may sound, I've learned that the biggest relationship you'll ever have, the hardest relationship you'll ever have, is the one with yourself. And that's the relationship I'm in now. I've learned that when you're lucky enough for someone to come along who loves you, then you have to accept it. It's all about acceptance, it's not about tolerance. It's about learning to be comfortable with the fact that someone can love you, it's about accepting the fact that you can love someone else, and when you do that it's fucking powerful. Before, I would think love was about tolerating this person, or tolerating that person. Love isn't about what someone can buy for you or how good a cook they are, love is about how that person can make you feel just by looking at you, just by holding your hand or laying their head on your chest.

When I think of previous loves, the biggest cost to me has been the fact that I destroyed people's lives. The hurt I caused those closest to me really doesn't sit well with me. You know, I like to project onto the world that I'm a cunt, but I'm not. It's a pretence designed to stop others getting too close. Even now, at fifty-six, after sixteen years of sobriety and working on myself, I still have real issues with intimacy. Sometimes I'd still rather you'd think I'm an awful person than get close and see just how scared and sensitive I am.

There's a moment first thing in the morning which is the most dangerous moment of the day for me. It's when thoughts can creep back in, thoughts like, *Oh today would be a good day to really fuck things up*. I've learned not to listen to that first thought and I right myself, get up and try my best to have a good day. Recovery doesn't have a time scale,

I've said it before, but uncommon sense is that voice in your head which will tell you to do the absolute opposite of what you should be doing. It doesn't say, 'You're in a loving relationship – this is what you've always dreamed of,' it says, 'You're in a relationship – ruin it.' And so the cost for me is to continuously keep that voice in check, but that cost is well worth it these days.

I was with Johnny for twelve years and he stood by me through thick and thin. He put up with things that no human being should ever have to put up with. When I met Johnny, he was like a gift from God, a blonde angel and a troubled soul, and that was what I was drawn to. There was something about him that was just everything. He had a face on him that was like innocence but he could have the temperament of the devil when he was pushed to it. He was like Luke Skywalker and I was Darth Vader, and I did everything I could to take him to the dark side.

In our relationship, like in so many other relationships, I never felt worthy, I never felt enough, I felt like I needed validation from absolute strangers, I felt like I needed to destroy the good in my life. We were in a three-way relationship: me, Johnny and addiction, and that's the way it's been for a lot of my relationships. And addiction came first, I'm afraid – how can anyone play second fiddle to addiction? When I started this book, I said that I had no regrets, and that's a major lie. Because although I have no personal regrets about what I've done to myself, I have so, so many when it comes to the people that I've hurt.

I'm drawn to a pigeon with a broken wing. I can't help it. It was the same with my last partner, David. He came to my house and I never wanted him to leave. I remember walking down the Embankment hand in hand with him, another blonde-haired, blue-eyed angel, on day three of him being there and I said to him, 'I'm going to make you love me. I'm going to make you fall in love with me.' And, of course, I did, but you know, that was probably the worst thing I could possibly have done to David because, even though I was in recovery, I still hadn't put the work in to love myself. We were together eight years, and what I learned in those eight years is that I can be just as destructive as I was twenty-eight years ago. But, relationships are relationships and they're the hardest fucking thing on the planet. David was another gift from God, but I'm slowly realising that, without continually putting the work in with myself, I can't be with anyone else. And so that's what I'll continue to do, because being in a loving and caring relationship with a partner is one of the biggest blessings on the planet.

I've learned that I'm blessed to have friends in my life, real friends. Friends that steer me and watch my back. Friends who sometimes I don't talk to for six months but then when I do talk to them, we're straight back on that page, but I also have friends that I speak to every day. You know, it's taken me fifty years to get real friends, friends who don't want anything apart from the best for me.

At the age of fifty-six, my relationship with my family is better than ever because they know they can trust me now – it was never a question of me trusting them, but to put your trust in me when I couldn't even trust myself was ridiculous. They know they can ask me a question now and I'll tell them the fucking truth. There's an honesty within my family which is beautiful now, I just don't need to lie anymore, I kind of lied about everything there was to lie about. Now, I've found this new thing, which is really fucking amazing, and just blows my mind. The truth.

I'm so lucky now that I have so many people in my life. Some of them have no careers and some have massive careers, it's not about what people do as a living, it's what they do for themselves and for you. For the first time in my life, I have friends who love me for who I really am. And sometimes, that can include me being a bit of a cunt still. I've learned that friendship is a two-way street. For a long time, I was driving around my own one-way system and didn't give a fuck about who had right of way. But now I've realised that friendship is about flow. It's about give and take, knowing wrong from right. Admitting when you're wrong. But always being right . . . You know even now, if I apologise, I still manage to make sure that I come out of it looking like I'm right. But my friends know that and accept it, and that's what friendship is about.

How do you learn to love yourself? I learned that you have to deal with the trauma of your past and understand how that can shape who you are and how you behave. The trauma I experienced as a ten-year-old child, which I thought I'd dealt with, I had never dealt with. I'd just carried it through life and let it get bigger and more harmful. There comes a point in life when you think you love yourself because you buy expensive clothes, or because you're in a job everyone loves you for, but that's like being thirsty and filling up a water tank and then shooting three bullets through it and letting it all drain away.

I think the big shift came in really learning to care about myself. I'd had thirty years of hating myself and using people and then when I had that shift of being able to love myself I was able to start loving other people.

Nothing I ever did was easy. Ever. If I'd listened, it would have been easy, but I didn't, because I had to do everything my way, I knew best. Every lesson I've learned, I've learned the fucking hard way. If there's a fork in the road and one's the easy way and one's the hard way, I'll still choose the hard way because that's the way I'm wired. To this day, if a sign says don't touch, then I'll touch it. If a sign says do not open this door, I'll open the door. You only need to dare me once.

I would do absolutely anything to repair the damage that I've done, and I'm doing everything I can, every day. I can't turn back time, and I try not to dwell on that. But what I can do is make today great and tomorrow even better. What I wish for the future is to continue to be of service whenever I'm needed. I'm always at the end of the phone if someone has a problem. I love life, and I want to carry on loving other people and continue to love myself. I want to continue to make people laugh and carry on laughing. You know, from a six-year-old kid running around the estate wearing a pair of plastic tits to my Instagram account now, I've always tried to make people laugh and always tried to make people love me. To laugh and to love, because really that's all I've ever wanted.

To be loved.

THINGS I'VE LEARNED WITH AGE

The main thing I've learned with age is never
to look your age.

I've learned to embrace age. I spent most of my life lying
about my age and then I hit fifty and I thought, you know
what, I've fucking survived and I should be proud of that. As
long as you don't look it. See above.

I learned never to act my age. I'm fifty-six and I don't act
like most fifty-six-year-olds, and I think that keeps me
excited about life. I definitely don't feel fifty-six, and I think
that's all about a state of mind.

I've learned wisdom with age. Before, people wouldn't even
ask me for the time because they knew I would lie. Now,
people come to me and ask me for advice and for help, and
that's come with age.

I've learned that left actually means left and right actually
means right, not the other way round.

I learned you should never let anyone tell you that you're too
old or young for something.

I've learned to listen to advice, but not to take other people's
opinions onboard. I've learned that other people's opinions
are theirs and not mine. They have nothing to do with me.

I've learned that you're always still learning, and you're
always still working stuff out. I always will be. I might have
that on my gravestone.

With Thanks

Right you bunch of cunts, that's your lot. I hope you've read this book and realised that my life is amazing now because of the things I don't do anymore, not solely because of the things I do. It might be obvious but it's what I choose to no longer have in my life that makes it brilliant.

At this stage of an autobiography, you normally finish the book with thanks – thank you to their mum, their boyfriend, their publisher, their friends, their editor and all the people that I couldn't have made it through the last fifty-odd years without, and without whom I couldn't have written this book. So, here you go . . .

Thank you to my parents, without whom I wouldn't be who I am today. Thank you Mikey for creating this book with me – for putting up with my mood swings and drama – without you none of this would ever have been a reality. Thank you to George O'Dowd for always being there and always being the voice of reason – I love you. To Gary Asden for being the light, to Del Murray for giving me the love and the courage to be who I am today. Thank you Kate for the love and friendship, Nadim Aoun for the continued love, support and hard work – fuck, you deserve a medal. Thank you to David Graham for all the years of support and love, and to the Graham family. Thank you to Pippa Davenport. Thank you to James Tailor, sorry could never even come close. Thank you Richard Habberley – what a ride, eh? to Lawrence Malice – thank you for all the opportunities, they didn't go unnoticed – and thank you for the bail money. To Lisa Allen for always being you, to Mark McKenzy – Edna – thanks for always nagging. To Elton and David for the love that you bring to this world. To my brothers Dean and Kevin for still speaking to me after all these years. Thanks to Doss for the tick, to Edward for always believing in me, thank you to Reggie and Tailor for showing me unconditional love. Thank you to Stratty, god knows where you are, thank you to Bev for always being there when I needed you, thank you Sam McKnight, thank you Myles Grimsdale, thank you Cozette McCreery, John G, Patrick, Gabby, Christian, Vicky Heller, Sue Tilley, Princess Julia, Wayne Shyers, to Penny Chequer, Davina McCall, Marc Jacobs, Kelly Osbourne, Danny Flower, the late Mark Herman, Neneh and Cameron, and to everyone who has been on this crazy journey with me. To Kyle De'Volle for being the sister I never had, to Ruth at Featherstone Cairns, Hannah Black and everyone at Coronet and Hodder, to Professor Gazzard and James Hand, to Zoe and Claire and everyone at Allington House – keep doing what you're doing you save lives. And last but not least thank you to Stavvy for the future.

It might also be appropriate for me to list the people I regret upsetting, too. I still wouldn't change the addiction, all of those stories, all that drama, it's made me who I am today and it's made this book. I would change upsetting (some) people. But that list would read like the Yellow Pages, so I'm sorry to anyone I've upset along the way. Especially that girl whose hair we cut off, I do still feel quite bad about that.

Most of my morals today come from my mistakes. I pretend I don't really have morals or scruples, but I have so, so, many, and that's why I believe in helping people, because if I hadn't been helped I'd be dead now. I sometimes come across as judgemental but it's only when I see myself in someone that I want to try and pull them from their own raging disco inferno before the roof caves in on them. What you put out, you get back. And I try to put out good vibes only these days. I have freedom, I have self-respect, I have love, I have happiness and I have laughter. Oh, and now I have a book. Who could ever ask for anything more?

Big Love,

Tony x

Once you believe, you're halfway there.

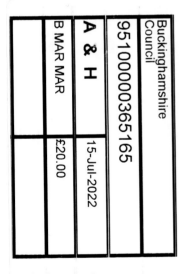

Buckinghamshire
Council

951000003365165

A & H

15-Jul-2022

B MAR MAR

£20.00

I don't take requests
6725653

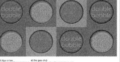